Cast

Cemil / Sergeant	George
Tamer	Philip A
Sebe	Brid Br
Serap	Rebecc
Filiz	Marianna Neofitou
Communist 1	Mehmet Ali Nuroglu
Haydar	Peter Polycarpou
Feride	Beatriz Romilly
Nare / Communist 2	Bita Taghavi

Creative & Production Team

Director	Mehmet Ergen
Designer	Neil Irish
Lighting Designer	Colin Grenfell
Assistant Director	Kate Moyse
Sound Designer	Adrienne Quartly
Costume Designer	Therese Steele
Production Manager	Roger Walpole
Stage Manager	Niki Edipidi
Assistant Stage Manager	Alex Constantin
Set Builder	Niall Bateson
Lighting Technician	David Salter
Technical Assistant	Paul Thomas
Press	Anne Mayer

For the Arcola Theatre

Artistic Director	Mehmet Ergen
Executive Producer	Leyla Nazlı
General Manager	Ben Todd
Assistant General Manager	Michael Harris
Finance Manager	Nicole Rosner
Associate Director	Serdar Bilis
Associate Producer	Philip Arditti
Front of House Manager	Alice Tatton-Brown
Front of House Manager	Gemma Greer
Technical Manager	Roger Walpole
Print Designer	Richard Scarborough

Biographies

Leyla Nazlı
Writer

Leyla gained a BSc Computing before co-founding Arcola Theatre in October 2000. After training at Birkbeck College in 'Writing for Stage' Leyla wrote *Silver Birch House*, which had a rehearsed reading at the Royal Court. Leyla was also one of the 50 writers chosen to take part in 'The Fifty', a year-long project with the BBC and the Royal Court Theatre to celebrate the 50th Anniversary of the Royal Court. Translations include Gogol's *The Government Inspector* and Kroetz's *The Nest*. Leyla is currently working on her second play *The King*.

Cast

George Antoni
Cemil / Sergeant

Trained at East 15 acting school; George went on to work with Lumiere & Son and Rational Theatre Company. Recent theatre includes *Resurrection Blues* (The Old Vic), Sherlock Holmes in *Trouble* (Manchester Royal Exchange). Film includes *Yes*, *Swept Away*, *Quills*, *The Man Who Cried*, *Elizabeth*, *Midnight Flight*, *Interview with the Vampire*, *Orlando*, *Greystoke* and *King Kong Lives*. Television includes *Hotel Babylon*, *The Magician of Samarkand* (Jackanory), *Poirot: Death on The Nile*, *Pompeii: The Last Day*, *Born & Bred*, *Lenny Blue*, *Lock Stock...*, *Gormenghast*, *The Bill*, *The Young Indiana Jones Chronicles*, *A Royal Scandal*, *Sharman*, *The Glam Metal Detectives* and *Space Virgins from Planet Sex*.

Philip Arditti
Tamer

Originally from Turkey, Philip trained at RADA. Theatre includes *A Family Affair* and *Tartuffe* (Arcola), *1001 Nights Now* (Nottingham Playhouse) and *Photos of Religion* (Theatre503). Television includes: *Whistleblowers*, *Caerddyd*, *Chopratown*, *Spooks* and *Casualty*. Film includes *Really* and *Chicken Soup*. Radio includes *Snow* (BBC4), *Sugar and Snow* (BBC3). Philip will also be appearing in *Pera Palas*.

Brid Brennan
Sebe

Theatre includes *Pillars of the Community*, *Rutherford and Son* (Olivier Award nomination), *Machine Wreckers* and *Man, Beast and Virtue* (National Theatre), *Macbeth* and *La Lupa* (Royal Shakespeare Company), *Absolutely! (Perhaps)* and *By the Bog of Cats* (Wyndham's), *Doubt* and *Dancing at Lughnasa* (Abbey Theatre Dublin, National Theatre and Phoenix Theatres London, Plymouth Theatre Broadway; Tony Award Best Featured Actress 1991–2), *The Cosmonaut's Last Message to the Woman He Once Loved in the Former Soviet Union*, *The Dark*, *The Little Foxes* (Olivier Award Nomination) and *A Kind of Alaska* (Donmar), *Woman & Scarecrow*, *Bone*, *Bailegangaire*, *Ourselves Alone* (Royal Court), *Juno and the Paycock* (Gaiety, Dublin), *Ten Rounds* (Tricycle Theatre), *Edward II* (Royal Exchange, Manchester), *Playboy of the Western World* and *The Shaugraun* (Druid Theatre, Galway), *Smelling a Rat* (Hampstead Theatre), *Holy Days* (Soho Poly), *Gold in the Streets* (Boston Theatre Co.). Film includes *Sunday*, *Topsy*

Turvy, Felicia's Journey, Dancing at Lughnasa (ifta Award, Best Actress 1999), *Trojan Eddie, St. Ex, Words Upon a Window Pane, She's Been Away, Hidden City, Ursula and Glenys, Anne Devlin, Maeve* and *Excalibur*. Television includes *Any Time Now, Cracker, Hedda Gabler, Tell Tale Hearts, Ghostwatch, The Birmingham Six, Itch, South of the Border, Four Days in July, The Daily Woman, Upline, The Billy Trilogy, Lorna, The Ballroom of Romance,* and *Bracken*. Radio includes *His Dark Materials, Twinkle Toes* and *Yerma*.

Rebecca Calder
Serap

Rebecca Calder is originally from County Durham and trained at The National Institute of Dramatic Arts, Sydney Australia. Feature film credits include Matthew Vaughn's soon to be released *Stardust, Cashback* directed by Oscar-nominated Sean Ellis. Theatre includes Sadler's Wells Theatre, Woodstock Theatre, and Up And Coming Shakespeare Company. And for television, work with award-winning Director Ivan Zacharias and Michael Jenkins for the BBC.

Marianna Neofitou
Filiz

Marianna is currently training at the Italia Conti Academy of Theatre Arts in all aspects of Dancing, Acting and Singing. Theatre includes, *Chitty Chitty Bang Bang* (London Palladium), *The Circle of Life, Witches of Eastwick* (Wimbledon Theatre). Television includes *Robinsons Fruit Shoot, SMTV Live The Brits 25, Christmas Rin and Comic Relief*. Film includes *Harry Potter 2 & 3*.

Mehmet Ali Nuroglu
Communist 1

Born in Istanbul, Mehmet Ali graduated from the Ankara State Conservatory in 2004. Theatre includes *Faust* and *Atcali Kel Mehmet* (METU Players), *Selim III* (Ankara State Theatre), *A Season in Hell* (IRZ Company) and *Macbeth* (HU Ankara State Conservatory). Mehmet Ali starred in the television series *Cemberimde Gul Oya* and *Kirik Kanatlar* (Broken Wings). Film includes *Waiting for Heaven* (dir. Dervis Zaim), *Zincirbozan* and *Fairy Dust* (currently in post production). Mehmet Ali also worked on the British-made short film *An Eye for a Tooth* (dir Murat Kebir). *Silver Birch House* is Mehmet Ali's UK debut.

Peter Polycarpou
Haydar

Peter's work includes award winning productions at both the RSC and National Theatre. Film includes *O Jerusalem, I Could Never Be Your Woman, De-Lovely, Oklahoma!* and *Evita*. Peter is best know for his part in *Birds of a Feather*. Television includes *The Bill, Eastenders, Casualty, Mile High, Holby City* and *Sunburn*. Peter is currently working on a pilot *Empathy* airing in May for the BBC. Theatre includes *Gizmo Love* (Actors Touring Company), *All the Ordinary Angels* (Royal Exchange Manchester), *Anna in the Tropics* and *Follow My Leader* (Hampstead Theatre), Arturo Ui in *The Resistible Rise of Arturo Ui* (The Bridewell), *The Odd Couple* and *Angels in America* (Manchester Library), *Titus Andronicus* (RSC). Musicals include original cast in *Oklahoma!* (National Theatre), *Les Miserables* (RSC) and *Miss Saigon*. The Phantom in

Phantom Of The Opera. Recently Peter also worked on the short film *Broken* directed by Vicki Psarias being shown by the East End London Film Festival. He wrote and produced his own short film *Mad George*.

Beatriz Romilly
Feride

Beatriz trained at Drama Centre London. Theatre credits include *Stars in the Morning Sky* (Union Theatre), *Mephisto*, *The Major of Zalamea* and *Spring Awakening* (Drama Centre). Played Beattie in *The Ghost Light* workshop directed by Di Trevis at the Old Vic. TV credits include *The Bill*, *Green Green Grass* (BBC) and *Doctors*.

Bita Taghavi
Nare / Communist 2

Bita completed her BA Hons in Acting at the Drama Centre, London in 2002. Whilst at college favourite roles included Liz Morden in *Our Country's Good,* Livia in *Women Beware Women*, and Marya Lebyatkin in *The Possessed*. On leaving college she worked for Half Moon Theatre Company playing Nina in *Cued Up*, which toured London and Wales. She has also taken part in a rehearsed reading for the John Caird Company and recently played the lead roles in two short films (one of which won the Greek International Short Film Competition and was shown on the BBC). Television includes *The Dress Woman of Turin* in the *Mummy Autopsy* series for the Discovery Channel. She recently finished a no.1 tour of *The Jungle Book* for the BSC, in which she played the roles of Raksha & Messua.

Creative Team

Mehmet Ergen
Director

Founding Artistic Director of both Southwark Playhouse (1993–9) and Arcola Theatre. Mehmet has won a variety of awards for these theatres including several Time Out Awards and Peter Brook Empty Space Awards. Directing credits include *Noises Off* (Frayn), *Much Ado About Nothing* (Shakespeare), *Roots* (Wesker), *Real Inspector Hound* (Stoppard), *The Nest* (Kroetz), *Fool For Love* (Sam Shepard), *Ashes to Ashes, One for the Road* (Pinter), *Lieutenant of Inishmore* (McDonagh), *Afterplay* (Friel, after Chekov). Mehmet has also won a number of awards and nominations for his directing and translations. His Arcola Credits include *Chasing the Moment* (Shepherd), *Seven Deadly Sins* (Brecht/Weill), *Release the Beat* (Johnson/Lewkowicz), *I Can Get It For You Wholesale* (Weidman/Rome), *Plebeians Rehearse the Uprising* (Gunter Grass). He also co-directed *Macbeth* with Jack Shepherd.

Neil Irish
Designer

Neil trained in Birmingham and later at The Slade. Recent projects include a UK tour of The Price for Compass Theatre Company, UK tour of *Vertigo* for Red Shift Theatre Company, *Woyzeck* at St. Ann's, New York, *Carmen* for Opera New Zealand, *I Pagliaci* for English Touring Opera, *Get Carter* UK tour for Red Shift, *Death of a Salesman* for Compass Theatre Company and Sheffield, and The National Opera Showcase at Hackney Empire. Opera includes productions at the Almeida/ENO

Festival, Opera Theatre Company Dublin, Holland Park Opera, Garden Opera and Opera North. Further theatre projects include productions at Birmingham Rep, Nottingham Playhouse, West Yorkshire Playhouse, Scarborough Theatres, Hull Truck, Pavilion Theatre Dublin, Gate Theatre London and Dublin, Royal Lyceum Edinburgh, Derby Playhouse, Greenwich Theatre. Neil has also worked for both set and costume departments at BBC Birmingham.

Colin Grenfell
Lighting Designer

Colin has recently lit *Rabbit* at the Old Red Lion and Trafalgar Studios in the West End, and the critically acclaimed *Black Watch* for the National Theatre of Scotland at last year's Edinburgh Festival and for its UK tour. Colin regularly lights productions for Improbable Theatre, including *Theatre of Blood* at the National Theatre in 2005 and *The Hanging Man* which premiered at the West Yorkshire Playhouse in May 2003 before touring the UK and abroad. Other work for them includes their 2001 show at the Royal Court Upstairs *Spirit,* and the UK and US hit *Lifegame*, as well as the multi-award-winning *70 Hill Lane*. Colin also lit Arcola's early hit show *Crime and Punishment in Dalston*.

Kate Moyse
Assistant Director

Studied B.A Philosophy (Bristol University) and M.A Fine Art (Slade,UCL). Kate has directed devised performances and short films and assisted theatre, documentaries and music videos. Directing credits include *Reserved for Others* (Transit Station, Berlin), *Monotony*

(Bloomsbury Theatre), *Frame the Punch* (CZKD, Belgrade), *How Did It All Go Wrong?* (Stanley Picker Gallery). Film screenings include *To Be is to Fit* (Nederlands Fotomuseum, Rotterdam and Novosibirsk State Art Museum, Russia), *Without a Bed* (Damaged Goods, Whitechapel Art Gallery), *Winston* (Anthology Films Archives, New York). Other screenings include *OPA (Paris)*, Institute of Contemporary Arts, Gallery 47 and The Brixton Art Gallery.

Adrienne Quartly
Sound Designer

Theatre includes *The Container*, (Edinburgh Fringe Festival 07), *Woyzeck* (St. Ann's Warehouse, Brooklyn NYC & Gate Theatre), *93.2FM* (Royal Court Theatre, London), *Playing For Time, A Touch Of The Sun* (Salisbury Playhouse), *Last Waltz Season* (Arcola), *Mercy Fine* (Clean Break Theatre), *Tejas Verdes* (Gate Theatre), *Hideaway* (Complicite), *Hysteria, Attempts On Her Life* (Battersea Arts Centre), *Jarman Garden, Inflated Ideas* (Riverside Studios), *Habeas Corpus, Quartermaine's Terms* (Royal Theatre, Northampton). Cellist: *Artist Rifles Piano Magic* (Rocket Girl Records), *National Alien Office* (Riverside Studios). Music Compiler for Gut Records.

Arcola Theatre

Arcola Theatre was founded in September 2000 when Mehmet Ergen (the present artistic director) and Leyla Nazlı converted a textile factory on the borders of Stoke Newington/Dalston into one of London's largest and most adaptable fringe venues. Arcola is now one of the country's most renowned fringe theatres with a distinct and powerful identity within both the local community and British theatre.

Since its foundation Arcola Theatre has won the Peter Brook Empty Space Award two years in a row and was given the Time Out Live Award twice for 'Inventive Programming on a Shoestring' in 2003 and 'Favourite Fringe Venue' in 2005/6. A large number of its productions have been selected as Critic's Choice in Time Out and the national papers. It has gained a reputation for staging work by some of the best actors, writers and directors including productions by William Gaskill, Dominic Droomgoole, Max Stafford-Clark, David Farr, Bonnie Greer, Adam Rapp, Sam Shepard, Eric Schossler, Helena Kaut-Howson and Kathryn Hunter.

In 2003 Arcola was said to 'live on love and hope rather than money' (*Independent*). Recently recognised as an 'Off-West End' rather than Fringe venue, Arcola now enjoys stable funding from, among others, Arts Council England. Nonetheless the ethos of an open door and endless possibilities keeps belts tight and life vibrant.

arcola
theatre

Historical Context

1909   Abdulhamid, the last Ottoman Sultan, is deposed by Young Turks

1914   Turkey enters World War I as an ally of Germany

1915   Sarikamis Campaign. Conflict during which hundred of thousands Armenians died during fatal deportations. This event is widely recognized as genocide by Western countries, yet the Republic of Turkey does not accept the deaths were the results of an intention from Ottoman authorities to indiscriminately eliminate Armenian people.

1919   Ataturk leads Turkish resistance in fight for sovereignty. War of Independence.

1923   Turkish state proclaimed with Ataturk as the President. Modernisation and secularisation of the state. Arabic script replaced by Latin alphabet, Turkish language revised, women's veil and fez banned. Exchange of population between Greece and Turkey.

1938   Dersim Rebellion against the Turkish state led by Alevi Zazas and Alevi Kurds from eastern Turkey. During the Ottoman period and early years of the Republic, the authorities had been unable to make people of Dersim recognise any authority other than their own. In 1936, Ataturk acknowledged Dersim as Turkey's most important interior problem. The rebellion took place as a result of oppressive government policies to 'Turkify' and control the region. Turkey mobilized 50,000 troops including the Turkish Air Force to suppress the rebellion and bombed the region. Retribution by Turkish forces claimed the lives of at least 40,000 people of Dersim, who were deported and massacred. Ataturk died, aged 57 on 10 November.

1960   May 16. Fearing that the founding principles of the Turkish Republic were being eroded by the Democratic Party, in power since 1950, the military staged the first coup.

1968   Many extreme leftist groups, mostly led by university students, take up arms. Some of these groups believe the revolution should start in the rural areas with the collaboration of peasants and workers.

1971   12 March. Following a series of unstable governments and with a growing revolutionary communist movement, a second military coup takes place. Several young student revolutionaries are hung.

1974   Amnesty for the 1971 military coup political prisoners.

1980   12 September. Mounting violence between Ultra-nationalists and Communist Revolutionaries end with the most violent military coup to date. The military stays in power for three years. Thousands of revolutionaries are imprisoned, tortured, killed and exiled. 'Turkey's left arm has been chopped-off'

1997   28 February. Following years of political and economical instability a coalition between a centre right party and a fundamentalist Islamic party leads to what came to be known as the peaceful 'Postmodern Coup'. Fighting between revolutionary groups (also Kurdish liberation guerrillas) and the army continue at a much milder level. The decade sees a series of hunger strikes in prisons, armed clashes in the east, the assassination of both leftwing journalists and rightwing businessmen, and bombs in the cities.

2002   An ex-fundamentalist Islamist politician Erdogan leads the Justice and Development Party (AKP) to an overwhelming victory in the elections.

2005   Nobel Prize winner Orhan Pamuk is put on trial for making the following statement: 'Thirty Thousand Kurds and a million Armenians were killed in these lands and nobody dares talk about it'. Charges were dropped a year later.

Zaza (an 'ethnicity')

The Zaza are an ethnic minority found in the eastern Anatolia region of Turkey. Most Zazas are Muslims; a minority being Sunni Muslim and the majority being Alevi (Muslim). Zazaki, the language spoken by Zaza people, is in the Indo-European language group with influences from Turkish. The exact size of the Zaza population is unknown but is estimated at 3 to 4 million.

As well as widespread suppression and wholesale evacuation of villages, the poor economic situation in eastern Turkey has forced the majority of the Zaza population to emigrate into Turkish or European metropoles: In the late 70s the livelihood of many Zazas from Tunceli (Dersim) were destroyed during clashes between the Turkish state and leftist revolutionary groups; later, in the 80s and 90s, Zazas from the rest of the country were forced into exile as a result of the guerrilla war between the Kurdish Workers Party (PKK) and the Turkish army. Many Zaza villages remain to this day eerily empty or are only inhabited by the elderly during the summer months.

Until the beginning of the 2000s, the public use of Zazaki was not legal. The consequences of this process of 'Turkification' combined with mass emigration abroad has resulted in substantial loss of the language – so much so that the younger generations hardly speak the language at all.

Alevi (a 'religion')

Alevi is a blanket term for a large number of different heterodox communities, whose actual beliefs and ritual practices differ much. It is practised mainly in Turkey, where Alevis are estimated to number 25 million. Alevis are denounced as 'pagan' by mainstream Muslims (Shia and Sunni), although some orthodox Alevis also denounce certain factions within Alevism. Their conception of Allah is varied. Though certain orthodox groups accept the idea of a creator, some factions believe that Allah is merely the good in humans.

The religion of the Alevis, though to some extent Islamicised, differs considerably from Sunni Islam. Prayer (Namaz), the fast in Ramadan, Zakat and the Hajj are alien practices to Alevi communities who do not pray in mosques. Instead they have their own religious ceremonies (Cem), officiated by 'holy men' (Dede) belonging to a hereditary priestly caste, at which religious poems (Nefes) are sung and, men and women carry out ritual dances (Semah). Many more elements of pre-Islamic Turkish and Iranian religions have been retained than among Sunni Muslims, and pilgrimages to sacred springs and mountains are especially common. Instead of adherence to the shari`a, Alevis profess obedience to a set of simple moral norms; they claim to live according to the inner (Batin) meaning of religion rather than its external (Zahir) demands.

My gratitude to those who helped shaping this play:
Mehmet Ergen, Rebecca Lenkiewicz, Tiffany Watt-
Smith, John Burgess, Serdar Bilis, Judith Johnson,
Irina Brown, Ben Todd and the actors who took part in
the production, workshop and readings.

Leyla Nazlı
May 2007

For the unnamed people

SILVER BIRCH HOUSE

First published in 2007 by Oberon Books Ltd
521 Caledonian Road, London N7 9RH
Tel: 020 7607 3637 / Fax: 020 7607 3629
e-mail: info@oberonbooks.com
www.oberonbooks.com

A catalogue record for this book is available from the British
Library.

Cover design: www.rscarborough.co.uk

ISBN: 1 84002 787 8 / 978 1 84002 787 7

Printed in Great Britain by Antony Rowe Ltd, Chippenham

Characters

HAYDAR, 47

SEBE, married to Haydar, 45

TAMER, their son, 18

FERIDE, their daughter, 17

SERAP, their daughter, 13

FILIZ, their daughter, 11

NARE, Haydar's sister, 24

CEMIL, married to Nare, 30

COMMUNIST 1, a male communist, 25

COMMUNIST 2, a female communist, 25

SERGEANT, Turkish Army Sergeant, 30

The following parts can be doubled:

NARE / COMMUNIST 2

CEMIL / SERGEANT / COMMUNIST 1

The action takes place between 1977 and 1980
in a small mountain village in Eastern Turkey.
The final scene takes place in Istanbul.

Act One

SCENE 1

Summer 1977. A silver birch wood and orchard in front of a small village house. HAYDAR and CEMIL are felling trees. They are surrounded by stumps, and some saplings, which remain untouched. CEMIL is wearing faded seventies bell-bottom trousers, which keep getting tangled up in the trees and caught under his shoes. HAYDAR's trousers are a more classic cut for a middle-aged peasant man. Both men are wearing hats and old jumpers. Also beyond the fence is HAYDAR's house, which is built of stone and mud and is almost hidden by trees. Though the style of the men's clothing is relatively up to date, the village is still without electricity and running water. SEBE, NARE, FILIZ and SERAP are in the kitchen, out of view. Between the house and the orchard are a table and two benches.

HAYDAR cuts the trees furiously. CEMIL is leaning on his axe. He is anxious.

CEMIL: I am really sorry Haydar.

HAYDAR: It's too late.

CEMIL: I thought…you said…

HAYDAR: I left you for just a few hours!

CEMIL: It was the biggest tree and I thought it would be a strong pillar to hold the roof of the house.

HAYDAR: I told you on day one. Cut as many as you need, but do not touch this one. Didn't I?

CEMIL: I forgot.

HAYDAR looks into CEMIL's eyes.

HAYDAR: How can you forget such a thing? How?

CEMIL is surprised, he puts his axe down and starts to leave.

Where are you going?

CEMIL: Haydar, I don't think I want to build a house now and I am sorry that I made you angry.

HAYDAR: You get back to your work before I cut your legs and use them as pillars for the bloody roof instead of my trees!

CEMIL panics, gets his axe and starts cutting. They don't talk for a while. SEBE comes out of the house and calls.

SEBE: Do you want something to drink before dinner?

HAYDAR: Get us some water.

SEBE: Filiz!

SERAP and FILIZ run out of the house and chase each other around the table.

SERAP: You'll never be able to catch me.

FILIZ: Yes I can.

SEBE: Stop it now. Here Filiz, take some water for your father and Cemil.

FILIZ: Why can't Serap take it?

SEBE: Serap is going to help Nare in the kitchen.

FILIZ takes the water to her father. SEBE and SERAP go to the kitchen. FILIZ pours the water and offers it to her father. HAYDAR takes the water and drinks.

HAYDAR: Tell your mother to feed the horse.

FILIZ leaves. HAYDAR refills the glass.

Have some water.

CEMIL's trousers drop from his waist, they keep getting tangled up in the trees and caught under his shoes. He pulls them up and struggles to hold them.

You know, one day rats will crawl up your leg and nest in your pubes.

CEMIL laughs, embarrassed.

What kind of trousers are they?

CEMIL: It's the fashion.

HAYDAR: You think that's why my sister was attracted to you?

CEMIL: Don't you think they suit me?

HAYDAR: They look ridiculous. Where did you get them anyway?

CEMIL: From the flea market.

HAYDAR: Couldn't you find anything decent?

CEMIL: They're called bell-bottoms.

HAYDAR: So they ring when you walk then?

CEMIL: Yes. All the sheep look at me when I walk.

HAYDAR: I hope you are not trying to attract the two-legged creatures with them as well.

CEMIL: These were the only pair of trousers I could afford in the flea market.

HAYDAR: Just as long as you're making my sister happy.

CEMIL: I promised, didn't I?

HAYDAR: You are a very lucky man Cemil.

CEMIL: I'm grateful to you, Haydar.

HAYDAR: Aah, don't be grateful to me.

Pause.

It takes a long time to grow these trees. And a long time to cut them down!

CEMIL: We should've had the chainsaw. I've heard that it swallows a whole week's work in one hour.

HAYDAR: My uncle has one, but he wouldn't lend it to me.

CEMIL: What, does he think we're going to eat it?

HAYDAR: He protects his tools like he protects his gold.

CEMIL: I would have loved to use it. What does it look like?

HAYDAR: How can you use it if you don't know what it looks like?

CEMIL: What's he making this time, our brilliant craftsman?

HAYDAR: Don't mock him. He's a very good carpenter.

CEMIL: Sorry, I forgot he's your uncle. I shouldn't talk like this.

HAYDAR: He's supposed to be teaching me how to make chairs. Have you seen the table and chairs I made? I made them from a whole walnut log. Sebe doesn't like them for some reason.

CEMIL: They are kind of crooked.

HAYDAR: Are you two ganging up on me?

CEMIL: How did your uncle learn to become a carpenter anyway?

HAYDAR: In the city. After the troubles in '38, when he was a kid. He worked for a carpenter there.

CEMIL: Where did you end up, back then?

HAYDAR: I didn't go anywhere. I stayed here. I hid in the mountains, with my father.

CEMIL: Your uncle must regret coming back here.

HAYDAR: Why?

CEMIL: He would have had his own shop by now.

HAYDAR: Shop? He couldn't have got himself a wife, let alone a shop.

CEMIL: I thought you said he was a great carpenter.

HAYDAR: He's four feet tall. Who's going to marry him? He's lucky he managed to find a decent wife here in the village. No one in the city would marry their daughter to one of us, let alone a midget. You know, they didn't even take him into the army. I did three years.

CEMIL: But army service is eighteen months.

HAYDAR: I was one of the exemplary soldiers. And my general liked me. He taught me how to read and write. He was a good man. I think he understood me.

CEMIL: So you were buddies.

HAYDAR: Yes I told him my life story. Then I fell in love with his wife and slept with her.

CEMIL: What?

HAYDAR laughs at CEMIL. Pause.

HAYDAR: Aha! That's the reason.

CEMIL: The reason for what?

HAYDAR: The reason why my uncle won't teach me how to make chairs. He was never a soldier and I was.

CEMIL: He doesn't know how lucky he is. I wish I never had to join the army.

HAYDAR: It gives you discipline, turns boys into men.

CEMIL: Are you saying your uncle is not a real man?

HAYDAR: Only his wife knows that.

Pause.

I remember when they all came back from the city. I was so excited, everyone was. After ten years who wouldn't be? Everybody was trying to find their relatives in the herd of people coming down the hill towards us. I immediately picked out my sister Kezban.

(*Thoughtfully.*) She was beautiful. The image of my mother!

CEMIL: I had a sister. We never found her.

HAYDAR: She could be in one of the orphanages. How old was she then?

HAYDAR starts working and tidying up.

CEMIL: She was four or five. Maybe she died. But we still think that one day she's going to appear from somewhere.

HAYDAR shouts out.

HAYDAR: Serap don't forget to pick up the branches from the road.

SERAP comes out of kitchen.

SERAP: Dad I am helping Mum in the kitchen.

HAYDAR: Then get Filiz to do it.

CEMIL: My brother searched the orphanages for my sister, but he had no luck.

HAYDAR: Let sleeping dogs lie.

CEMIL rolls a cigarette. He sits on the floor.

When are you going to quit? I didn't let you marry my sister so she would end up a widow.

CEMIL: I'll do the rest first thing in the morning.

HAYDAR: Don't bother. You rest. Just enjoy killing yourself in my paradise.

SERAP is dragging FILIZ out of the house behind her.

FILIZ: Let go of me.

SERAP: Mum! Dad asked her to pick up the branches and she is not doing it.

FILIZ: Do it yourself.

SERAP: But I am helping Mum.

FILIZ: Why can't I help Mum, why does it always have to be you telling me what to do?

SEBE comes out of the house carrying bowls to set the table for dinner.

SEBE: You two. Stop fighting. Filiz, go and help your dad.

FILIZ: I won't.

SERAP: Dad. Filiz is not listening to you!

HAYDAR: Filiz get here now!

FILIZ: You are a bitch Serap.

SERAP: You wouldn't say that unless you were a bitch yourself.

FILIZ: You wouldn't say that unless you were a bitch yourself.

SEBE: Will you two stop it. You are going to make your father angry again.

HAYDAR: Filiz!

SEBE: Go before he drags you by the hair.

FILIZ: All right, all right!

She pushes past SERAP.

SERAP: I'll…

SEBE: Serap that's enough!

SERAP: But Mum…

SEBE: Ssssh! You are older then her. Go and peel the potatoes.

SERAP goes back to the kitchen. NARE comes out. She is pale.

SEBE: How are you now?

NARE: I thought the sickness stopped after they started to move.

23

SEBE: Some women have morning sickness for nine months.

SEBE and NARE go back into the house.

CEMIL: I think I should go and wash in the stream. I smell like a billy-goat.

HAYDAR: You should wash up with hot water in the house.

CEMIL: I don't want to bother the ladies.

HAYDAR: It's their job. Sit. They'll call us when dinner's ready.

CEMIL sits down and continues smoking.

HAYDAR: Look at that little one; (*He gestures at a small tree.*) in ten years it'll be like the ones we've just cut down. Every one of these trees is like a child to me.

CEMIL: I smell food.

HAYDAR: They'll call us when it is ready. This one for instance was six years old. (*He gestures at a tree-stump.*)

CEMIL: How do you know that?

HAYDAR: Count the rings.

CEMIL counts the rings of another tree.

CEMIL: The one I cut was thirty-five years old.

HAYDAR: The tallest tree in the orchard.

CEMIL: It took me two hours. The bastard.

HAYDAR: I could kill you right now.

CEMIL: Why did you want to keep this tree?

HAYDAR: Because it's mine.

CEMIL: This tree is thirty-five years old. It was here before you lived here.

HAYDAR: I said I planted it.

CEMIL: Thirty-five years ago? You built this house ten, fifteen years ago.

HAYDAR: Are you calling me a liar?

CEMIL: No, no, but…

HAYDAR: But what?

CEMIL: Forgive me. I am not trying to argue with you.

HAYDAR: Good.

CEMIL: I think I'll go and give Sebe and Nare a hand.

HAYDAR: You are a man. Men don't cook. Men don't work in the kitchen like wives.

CEMIL calls NARE. She comes out of the house.

CEMIL: Nare heat some water!

NARE: Why?

CEMIL: Because I need to wash.

HAYDAR: Good!

Let me tell you a story, but listen carefully.

CEMIL sniffs, doesn't really encourage him, but HAYDAR continues anyway. CEMIL lights another cigarette and crosses his arms. He sits uneasily.

Once upon a time, there was a thief, the most hated and wanted thief in the country, who travelled from one city to another, robbing and stealing from the old and the young, until eventually, one day he was caught. In the prison, he decided that from now on, he was going to become a decent honest man and that perhaps, if he did only good things, he would go to Heaven when he died. After a long time, the thief was released, and he started the long journey back to his old village. He was almost there when he passed a little house on a small hill in the middle of a barren field. Suddenly, he saw this middle-aged man

25

running towards him across the field, waving his arms around.

SEBE comes out of the house with bread for the table, speaks, and then returns to the kitchen.

SEBE: The dinner is almost ready.

HAYDAR: So the thief stopped and asked the man 'What is the matter?'

CEMIL: They are calling us.

HAYDAR: We'll sit down in a minute. And the man, who was very out of breath, said 'I've been waiting for someone to pass on this road for a long time. I have to ask you a question.' So the thief said 'Go ahead, what is the question?'

NARE brings out an aluminium jug full of water and a plastic washing-up bowl. She puts it on the ground near the men.

NARE: The hot water is ready Cemil.

CEMIL gets up to leave. HAYDAR stops him. NARE goes back to the house.

HAYDAR: We'll wash in a minute. And the man said 'I have this vineyard; I've been looking after it for years and I was wondering, is it right for me to be the first person to taste a grape from my vineyard?'

CEMIL sits down again.

And the thief thought for a minute, and said 'Yes, yes of course. It's your vineyard, and you looked after it for years. So you should be the first to taste its fruit.'

SEBE brings a pan of soup from the house, puts it on the table, speaks and returns to the house.

SEBE: The soup is going to get cold.

HAYDAR: I said we're coming.

SEBE: Don't blame me for serving you cold soup.

HAYDAR: Heat it up again woman!

Anyway, the man looked very pleased, and shook the thief's hand, and said 'Thank you very much. May God make your way safe.' And with that, the man turned and hurried back towards his house. But then the thief realised that there was no vineyard, only barren fields. And so he called back the man, and asked; 'Where is the vineyard? I'm curious. I want to see it.' And the man said 'The vineyard is my daughter.' The thief didn't know what to do. Should he just close his eyes to the man's desire, and walk past, or, should he do something about it, and get his reward in heaven? Well he didn't need to think much. He picked up a big rock and killed the man right there.

CEMIL finishes his cigarette and looks at the garden. Silence.

He lights another one.

So my question is, should the thief go to heaven after killing that kind of man, or not?

CEMIL: God, I don't know Haydar. You know I am not a clever man.

SERAP brings spoons from the house, puts them on the table and goes over to the men. She brings the hot water and washing bowl closer to HAYDAR. He wedges the bowl between his feet. SERAP pours the water onto his hands. He first washes his hands and then his face. SERAP then does the same for CEMIL. As they wash, the men talk. FILIZ comes from the garden. HAYDAR notices her.

HAYDAR: Bring the towel and soap Filiz.

FILIZ: Ow! Look at my hands! I can hardly close them and they're all cracked. Can you do it Serap?

SERAP: Oh stop complaining.

FILIZ: They really, really hurt.

27

LEYLA NAZLI

SERAP: Mine too. Can't you see my hands are full?

SEBE hands FILIZ a towel, which she gives to HAYDAR. He dries his hands with the towel and gives it back to FILIZ, who goes and stands next to SERAP and waits for CEMIL to finish washing so she can hand the towel to him. SEBE and NARE serve the soup at the same time. They sit for the dinner.

CEMIL: Did you pack the bags Nare?

NARE: Yes.

HAYDAR: You're going?

CEMIL: We've cut down the trees we needed.

HAYDAR: You can stay here as long as you want you know that.

CEMIL: Thank you. We're going to stay with my brother for a while.

HAYDAR: Baran has invited me to his house tomorrow night. Why don't you come with me?

A dog barks.

Serap did you feed the dog?

CEMIL: I heard he drinks a lot. I don't drink myself, as you know.

SERAP picks up her plate.

HAYDAR: I don't either, but sometimes, it's nice to drink.

SEBE: Not your food Serap.

SERAP: I don't want it any more.

SEBE: Serap go get Mancho's food from the kitchen and eat yours.

CEMIL: People don't like him.

FILIZ: I like him.

SERAP: You like Baran?

28

FILIZ: No.

NARE: They are not talking about the dog Filiz.

SEBE: Baran? Dog? I don't see the difference.

HAYDAR: People around here don't like anyone who has land and money.

CEMIL: He's got more land than everybody else in this village.

SEBE: While our children are wasting away, chasing a few animals in the mountains.

HAYDAR: All I know is he's a funny man and I have a good time with him.

Did Fat Metin accept the job?

CEMIL: I don't know. I only asked him once.

HAYDAR: You have to finish everything before winter and you can't afford to build a crooked house. You are starting in two weeks. He is a very good bricklayer. I'll talk to him tomorrow. You're a lucky man. Do you know that?

CEMIL: Yes I do.

HAYDAR: When I built this house there was no one to help me.

SEBE: The Village Committee told you not to build the house here. The ground was rocky. But you went off and did it anyway. Even your own father wouldn't come and help.

HAYDAR: If even my own father wouldn't help me then what could I expect from the Village Committee?

FILIZ: Dad would you like a cup of tea?

HAYDAR: No! I want no tea.

SEBE: Don't lose your temper again. We are just talking.

HAYDAR: It's too late now. Once you start poking about in a beehive, you'd better expect a sting! Anyway, I was strong enough to do it on my own.

SEBE: You are mad!

HAYDAR: All you do is nag. Tell me one little thing you enjoyed, when we built this house?

SEBE: We were staying in a tent by a building site for six months. What was there to enjoy?

CEMIL laughs unexpectedly.

NARE: What's so funny?

CEMIL: I just thought you could have built the house somewhere else.

SEBE: May your tongue be pink and healthy for the rest of your life. I beg you, say that again.

HAYDAR: (*He imitates her.*) I beg you say that again. Yes I could have built the house somewhere else, but it wouldn't be as strong as this. This house won't move an inch, even if there is an earthquake. You don't have a clue about how the world works, none of you! Can't you just say one nice thing?

SERAP: Come on, just say one nice thing Mum!

FILIZ: Did we miss the radio play?

SEBE: Our life is a play.

HAYDAR: And you are the star.

SEBE: How many snakes did you kill?

FILIZ: Ohh! Snakes?

HAYDAR: You are talking as if you went through hell.

SEBE: It was. Sometimes I wanted to hold my hand over Serap's mouth.

SERAP: To kill me?

SEBE: No, not to kill you. To keep the snakes away. You were small enough to sleep in our bed, but I had to think about

Feride and Tamer too. It was so dark. They were coming from everywhere. Once a snake came into our bed and your father smothered it with the quilt. They were drawn in by your cries!

FILIZ: God. I am glad I wasn't born in a tent.

HAYDAR is staring at the garden. He doesn't talk. CEMIL starts smoking. NARE and the others tidy up the table.

HAYDAR: Where have Tamer and Feride been all this time?

SEBE: Filiz, ask your father if he wants some tea.

FILIZ pulls a face as if she doesn't understand her mother.

FILIZ: Dad do you want some tea?

HAYDAR: (*He's upset with SEBE.*) If she lets me drink my tea in peace.

He looks at everyone. There is silence at the table.

Ok, go ahead then, but make sure it's brewed well. (*He holds FILIZ's face and turns it to CEMIL.*) That's my black calf. She looks like our black calf, she has the same eyes. (*Laughs.*) Big and black! I think Sebe was looking at our black bull when Filiz first moved in her tummy.

FILIZ doesn't like the comparison.

FILIZ: Is that why you killed him?

HAYDAR: Yes, I was jealous; I couldn't stand the sight of that animal.

FILIZ: You promised me that you wouldn't touch him.

HAYDAR: What can you do with a bull that has a bad back? (*To CEMIL.*) He fell down the waterfall while he was chasing the cows.

(*To FILIZ.*) We can't keep bulls with bad backs that can't… you know…during the season…

31

FILIZ: Ughh Dad!

She exits, SERAP exits with her.

SEBE: Nare's baby moved today for the first time.

CEMIL: Really?

NARE: It moved when you felled that big tree.

CEMIL: Oh he is going to be a boy.

SEBE: This baby is going to be trouble. How long has it been?

NARE: I never knew that babies jumped like this.

SEBE: They do all sorts of things; they knock, they kick…

CEMIL: Even my son agrees that we need a strong tree for the house.

SEBE: Where are they? They've never been this late.

FILIZ: (*FILIZ and SERAP come out with tea.*) I work more than them.

HAYDAR: Next year you'll be old enough to work in the field. How old are you now?

FILIZ: I don't know. Ask Mum.

SEBE: You're ten.

FILIZ: I'm not ten. You don't even know my age.

SEBE: I don't even remember what I had for lunch yesterday.

FILIZ: Dad, you must know how old I am.

HAYDAR: Nine.

FILIZ: Aunt Nare?

NARE: Sorry Filiz, I don't even know my age, my mum used to say I was born when the cows gave birth.

FILIZ: I am eleven.

HAYDAR: (*To SEBE.*) Is she eleven?

SEBE: She is if she says so.

NARE: My God, in three or four years time you'll be married too.

FILIZ: Serap is before me. She'll get married first.

SERAP: I'm never getting married.

CEMIL: Then you will be a spinster.

SERAP: What's wrong with being a spinster?

NARE: There's nothing wrong with being a spinster. I wouldn't marry if I had a choice. You wait until you find someone you want to marry.

SEBE: I wish you were all boys. There is no future for girls around here.

SERAP: You always say that. It's your fault that we're girls.

FILIZ: I don't want to be a boy.

SERAP: (*In a low voice as if she doesn't want HAYDAR to hear.*) Because you want to marry Bulent, is that why?

FILIZ: Why do you always say things that you really want for yourself?

SERAP: I don't want anything. One day, when I grow up, I'll leave this place.

HAYDAR: You don't know how hard it is.

SERAP: Yes I do.

SEBE: You don't know the life in the mountains.

SERAP: Who said I was going to the mountains?

HAYDAR: And don't think that people will welcome you and give you food when ever you knock on their door. You don't know how hard it is living in fear. Not only of the

33

soldiers, but also of bears and wolves. You have to keep moving around, keep changing your position; especially in the winter.

SEBE: Your father didn't even have a pair of shoes, his feet bled. He couldn't even walk. Sometimes in the mountains they wouldn't find any food for a whole week. They would eat grass.

HAYDAR: Leave the past in the past. We should look to the future.

Blackout.

SCENE 2

Half an hour later. FERIDE and TAMER are back from the field, eating. They both are very exited. The others are having their tea.

NARE: Thanks for bringing the tomatoes Feride.

FILIZ: I planted them.

FERIDE: Comrades helped us all day. Did you notice the tall one Tamer? What was his name? He didn't even take a break.

HAYDAR sips his tea and looks out into the garden.

TAMER: Steel Hand. He's new. I haven't seen him before.

NARE: Steel Hand. What kind of name is that?

FERIDE: Oh they all have fake names. No one knows their real names.

CEMIL: These comrades, do you know who they are?

TAMER: Some of them come from the cities and some are from villages around here.

CEMIL: Do they have guns?

FERIDE: They have books. Lots of books.

CEMIL: Strange people.

FILIZ: I am going to join them when I'm fifteen. We are all going to Russia together.

HAYDAR: And what will you do there, Filiz?

FILIZ: We are going to be happy there, really happy. They say they are going to take all of us there. Isn't that right Tamer?

HAYDAR: They should get jobs in the city, instead of working in the fields for no money.

FERIDE: They're not after money. They're just helping Dad.

HAYDAR: Don't they have anything better to do?

TAMER: You don't think working in the field is good enough?

NARE: Comrades. What does it mean?

TAMER: It means brothers in arms. Friendship!

HAYDAR: You don't know who these people are. They're strangers.

CEMIL: Yeah! What are they after in these villages Tamer? If I were them, I'd stick to the cities. Everything is happening there. Nothing happens here.

TAMER: They're students who want to educate peasants. That's all.

HAYDAR: Think. Always think before taking a step.

CEMIL: Your father has a point there Tamer.

HAYDAR: Have you noticed how often salesmen visit the village lately?

FILIZ: A salesman gave us money.

HAYDAR: What?

SERAP: Me and Filiz were washing our hands in the stream after weeding the allotment. Filiz cut this tall grass and we were playing with it. And this salesman was passing through…

FILIZ: He bought the grass off me.

SERAP: He gave us ten lira.

HAYDAR: Tell me what exactly happened.

SERAP: I just told you.

HAYDAR: Did you ask him for the money?

FILIZ: No we didn't. He just gave it to us.

HAYDAR: Yes, yes, but why?

SERAP: I don't know. He said if I give you this money will you give me that grass, and Filiz said yes.

HAYDAR: What did you do with the money?

FILIZ: We gave it to Mum.

SEBE: But you didn't tell me anything about the grass.

HAYDAR: You are so naive sometimes!

CEMIL: Serap, did he ask you for more grass?

SERAP: Yes and he asked me where I got it from and I told him. He said he was in hurry and he'd come back for more some other time.

HAYDAR: What sort of salesman was he?

FILIZ: He didn't have a donkey like the other salesmen do.

CEMIL: Did he have a suitcase? With lots of things hanging from it?

SERAP: No. I asked him what he was going to do with the grass. He said he was going to smoke it, because he had run out of tobacco.

HAYDAR: Never do that again Serap, NEVER. You too Filiz, do you understand?

FILIZ: But Dad it was just grass. We would've given it to him for free, but when he offered us the money we didn't say anything.

HAYDAR: From now on you don't talk with the salesmen unless your mother is around ok? You can't trust anyone these days Tamer. We don't know who is who. Salesmen or comrades they are all the same to me. If they want to spy on each other, then let them do that in the city.

SEBE: Are you listening to your father Feride?

HAYDAR: This is an historical moment. Even your mother agrees with me.

SEBE: Because it's the truth.

HAYDAR: You can't change things by working in the fields with peasants. Why aren't they asking for money? That's the real question.

TAMER: All you think about is money. You think nothing can be achieved without money.

NARE: That's a fact, isn't it?

TAMER: No it's not Aunt Nare. We don't have any money. No one does in this village. But we have always survived without it. Money is not important.

CEMIL: Then what are they fighting for?

TAMER: For the Unity.

HAYDAR: Unity?

CEMIL: What?

TAMER: Unity of all the workers.

CEMIL: Which workers?

HAYDAR: Against whom?

TAMER: Against the injustice of the regime.

HAYDAR and CEMIL look at each other. They don't understand TAMER.

HAYDAR: Regime? Tamer you don't understand.

TAMER: You're right Dad, I don't understand, but they are teaching. Uncle Cemil, they have come here to educate us. We all need to learn. We need to read. I never thought about reading before. I didn't know what to read. We don't have books. Don't even get a newspaper. These people are risking their lives to help us. We don't just work. We talk as we work. We talk about other countries, the revolutions that have happened in the world. The leaders, the great thinkers who have changed everything in the world! Then we read books together. For the first time in my life I feel I'm learning something.

FERIDE: They told us about a man called Hitler who killed all the Jews and turned them into soap. Isn't that awful Dad?

SEBE: But they are terrible people those Jews.

FERIDE: How do you know Mum?

SEBE: Ask your dad if you don't believe me.

HAYDAR: I've never met one.

SEBE: I heard about them in the city. They snatch children. Then they put them in cradles that are made of needles. They wait until all the blood is drained from the body and then they drink it! They're terrifying. Jews, Caucasians, they are all the same.

SERAP: Do any of them live near us?

CEMIL: Don't worry. They're nowhere near here.

FILIZ: Where do they live then?

Silence. They look at each other.

FILIZ: Dad?

HAYDAR: (*Sarcastic.*) Ask Tamer he knows everything.

TAMER: Have you ever met them Mum?

SEBE: No. God forbid. I am telling you, they eat children.

HAYDAR: That's what they say about you Armenians too.

SEBE: What are you talking about?

SERAP: Dad, is Mum Armenian?

SEBE: No. Your father enjoys mocking me and my family.

FILIZ: What time is it?

HAYDAR turns on the radio. The radio beeps for the news.

We've missed the play again!

HAYDAR: Shhhh!

RADIO: This is the nine o'clock news. Two terrorists have been killed and four captured near the Eastern Border. During the operation, which started yesterday at three in the afternoon and continued until ten o'clock this morning, twenty bombs, eight Kalashnikovs, five rockets and a significant amount of explosives were recovered. One of the dead terrorists, going by the alias Footless, is known to have been involved in militant student groups. Those captured are presently under interrogation.

Thirty-five people are dead and forty seriously injured following a collision between two coaches on the highway near Istanbul. An eye-witness claimed that the accident was caused by a race which started when one coach driver attempted to overtake the other.

Silence.

TAMER walks out. HAYDAR is looking at the garden through the window. Lights fade out slowly.

SCENE 3

Late spring 1979. Around noon on a stormy wet day. A rocky hill with some small patches of grass. SERAP and FERIDE are guarding a herd of goats and sheep. They are both very cold.

SERAP: Let's take them home. It's not going to stop raining.

FERIDE: You can't take them home every time it rains.

SERAP: But they're not eating anything. I think they are even colder than us.

FERIDE: Don't be stupid. They have lots of wool on them.

SERAP: So how come they're not moving? I'm cold.

FERIDE: You have to learn to stay with the animals whether it's cold or wet.

SERAP: How do you do it?

FERIDE: You just think about something else.

SERAP: Ok.

Pause.

FERIDE: And?

SERAP: I'm thinking.

FERIDE: Good.

They are both shivering.

SERAP: I can't think about anything else.

FERIDE: Try harder.

SERAP thinks hard.

SERAP: I'm in a warm bed with a cup of rosehip tea. Aren't your hands freezing? I don't understand how you can knit in this weather.

FERIDE: You will when you grow up.

SERAP: I'm fifteen. (*Pause.*) Look, there are two men on the hill.

FERIDE: Where?

SERAP: There. I think it's them Feride.

FERIDE: Who? Where?

SERAP: There look. Did you see them?

FERIDE: No.

SERAP: You missed them. They've disappeared behind the hill.

FERIDE: It was probably just salesmen.

SERAP: No, they didn't look like salesmen.

FERIDE: Do you think it was Steel Hand?

SERAP: I'm not sure.

FERIDE: What? Either you saw him or you didn't?

SERAP: I did, but they were walking so quickly. Is that for him? (*Knitting.*)

FERIDE: Don't tell Mum ok?

SERAP: Is he nice?

FERIDE: He talks very beautifully.

SERAP: What does he talk about?

FERIDE: All sorts. Once he recited a poem, by this poet who was exiled to Russia, with his eyes closed.

She recites it, with her eyes closed.

> Comrades if I die before that day,
> It looks like it anyway,
> Bury me in a village in Anatolia.
> And if it's not too much trouble,
> I'd like a plane tree on my grave;
> Don't bother with a stone.

I kept wishing that that moment would never stop. Then he opened his eyes and he winked at me.

SERAP: Really?

FERIDE: Do you know I bet they went to Aunt Nare's house if they've gone that way. Can you see the big flag painted on the hill?

SERAP: There's some writing under it. What does it say?

FERIDE: 'I am Turkish and I am proud.'

SERAP: How do you know that? You can't read.

FERIDE: Dad told me when he took me to the dentist.

SERAP: Are we Turkish then?

FERIDE: I suppose so.

SERAP: Filiz reports me to the teacher when I don't speak Turkish at home.

FERIDE: That's how everybody learnt it.

SERAP: I can't help it if I forget sometimes. The teacher smacks me in front of the whole class. It's embarrassing. I catch Filiz talking to Mum in Zaza sometimes; I don't go and tell on her.

FERIDE: That's because you need to protect her.

SERAP: (*Proud.*) Because I'm older?

FERIDE: Yes.

They shiver as they talk.

SERAP: So if I walk towards the flag on that hill I'll get to the town without getting lost?

FERIDE: Yes. It is only three and a half hours' walking.

SERAP: Three and a half hours. Are there any wolves and bears?

FERIDE: Yes. If you walk there they will eat you alive.

SERAP: Have you ever seen one?

FERIDE: Once I was bitten by a wolf and now I can become a wolf whenever I want.

She imitates a wolf howling and scares SERAP, who tries to back away from her.

SERAP: Stop it.

FERIDE: You crack me up, you get scared so easily.

SERAP: Mum says spirits can appear in human shape. I sometimes think maybe you are not Feride at all, maybe you are a ghost. Or maybe I am not here at all, I'm just dreaming. Feride?

FERIDE: What?

SERAP: Are you really Feride?

FERIDE: You are such a silly girl.

FERIDE tickles her. SERAP giggles.

Do you feel warmer now?

SERAP: No! I think we should go to Aunt Nare's house.

FERIDE: We can't leave the animals here.

SERAP: We'll take them with us.

FERIDE: There'll be fields near the houses. The animals will go on the rampage through them and then the owners will complain to Dad. You can imagine what'll happen then.

SERAP: Don't you want to see Steel Hand?

FERIDE: We don't even know if it was them you saw.

SERAP: But what if it was? Don't you want to show him the shawl you are knitting for him?

She thinks for a while.

43

FERIDE: Let's go.

SERAP gathers the sheep, looking in the direction of the town.

SERAP: Are there buses in town?

FERIDE: Of course?

SERAP: Have you seen them?

FERIDE: No, but I know there are buses. Come on, I thought you were cold?

They both have sticks in their hands to gather the animals. While FERIDE guides the herd SERAP looks at the road, which leads to the town.

SCENE 4

Same day, late afternoon. SEBE is carding wool. There is already some ready for knitting. There are piles of woollen socks on the floor at her feet. TAMER comes in.

SEBE: Tamer, please get me a glass of water.

She leans back.

Ahh. My back is killing me.

TAMER: You've been sat in that same position since this morning. Why don't you take a break?

SEBE: I haven't cooked. Are you hungry?

TAMER: I had some bread and butter.

SEBE: Feride will cook something when she comes back. What do you want for dinner?

TAMER: Nothing special.

TAMER brings a cushion and places it behind SEBE.

Sit straight like this.

SEBE: Ahh this summer is going to be busy. I won't have a minute to myself. No time to eat, no time to cook. I need to knit at least thirty socks and ten jumpers before winter and the wool isn't good this year. Thank God Feride learnt how to knit.

TAMER: There's plenty here. (*He picks up some black wool.*)

SEBE: That's goat's wool. It's for rugs, for Feride's dowry. You can't wear that. It would destroy your beautiful skin.

TAMER: I am a tough man. (*He shows her his muscles.*)

SEBE: Oh no wonder Kahraman's daughter is coming around all the time.

TAMER: Was she here today?

SEBE: She brought some artichokes.

TAMER: Which one?

SEBE: The older one.

TAMER: That's nice of her.

He picks up the wool spinner on the floor and starts spinning.

What would people say if they could see me doing this?

SEBE: They would be jealous that their sons don't help them the way you help me. She also brought these gloves, here try them.

He tries them on and takes them off.

TAMER: The younger sister is the beauty.

SEBE: Well go for her then.

He gets up, puts his jacket on. He holds her face in his hands.

TAMER: For you I would marry all the girls in this village.

SEBE: Where are you going?

TAMER: To the meeting.

SEBE: What meeting?

TAMER: We have a meeting with the comrades.

SEBE: Tamer, be careful.

TAMER: Mum it's just a meeting. Tell Dad I'll finish chopping the wood tomorrow.

SEBE: Take care. Please. Please. Do you hear me?

TAMER: I hear you. Mum? What is it?

SEBE: Nothing. Everything.

TAMER: What? Tell me.

SEBE: You think you're invincible don't you? Immortal. Nobody's safe.

TAMER: I've got to go.

He starts to leave.

SEBE: I remember like it happened yesterday. I was five I think. What if starts all over again?

TAMER: Mum don't worry, you just have to not think about it.

SEBE: We were in a place that looked like a school, filled with people, hundreds of people, crammed in like sheep, waiting to be distributed to different cities. I don't remember how many days we were there. It was very hot. One afternoon everybody was taken into the street. We were made to stand in two rows, opposite each other, one on either side of the street. Behind us there were soldiers, guarding us, making sure we didn't run away. We were waiting for something. We waited and waited. (*Transfixed now, staring, as if seeing the soldiers walking in to town.*) And then we saw soldiers entering the town, and marching down the street, towards where we were standing. As they got closer, we saw that they were carrying three heads on sticks. It was Kopo and his two wives. The girls were so young. They both had long braids and I fell in love with

46

their hair right there. It didn't matter to me that they didn't have their bodies. They still had their beautiful dark, long hair. I heard someone from the crowd saying quietly, 'that is Seray'. For years I prayed to God for long and beautiful hair like theirs, and wanted to be called Seray.

TAMER kisses SEBE and leaves.

SCENE 5

Two hours later, FERIDE and SERAP have arrived home, and taken off their wet clothes. SEBE is drying SERAP's hair.

SERAP: You're hurting me Mum.

SEBE: Stay still.

SERAP: But you're hurting me

SEBE: I've got chores to do.

SERAP: Mum did you know where we went today?

SEBE: To the mountains?

FERIDE tries to stop SERAP talking but SERAP can't see her.

SERAP: Yes, but from there, to Aunt Nare's house.

SEBE: You went that far Feride?

SERAP: It's not really that far, and I saw the flag on the hill before the town.

SEBE: Well how is Nare?

FERIDE: She said hello.

SERAP: She baked us some bread, but we didn't eat it. We brought it for you. Feride was hoping to see Steel Hand, but…

FERIDE: Shut up Serap.

SEBE: Who?

FERIDE: Uncle Cemil took Ayse to the doctor.

SEBE: Is she ill?

SERAP: She doesn't speak?

SEBE: What?

FERIDE: Aunt Nare said she only stares at you.

SEBE: Is she deaf?

SERAP: Aunt Nare thinks she can hear her.

SEBE: I knew there was something wrong with that child. I remember the day she moved in Nare's tummy. It was too early, it wasn't the right time.

FERIDE: Their house is so nice. I wish our house was like that.

SERAP: Mum it was so exciting to see the trees me and Filiz peeled.

HAYDAR rushes in. He is very angry.

Dad I know the way to the town.

He slaps FERIDE suddenly and goes towards SERAP to slap her too, but SEBE stops him.

HAYDAR: The goats are eating the trees!

SEBE: They must have escaped from the barn.

HAYDAR: What do you expect, they're hungry! Why did you bring them home so early?

SEBE: It was raining.

HAYDAR: People don't take their animals home just because it's raining.

FERIDE and SERAP go out.

SEBE: The girls were soaking wet.

HAYDAR: You've spoiled them. They are eating the bark from my new trees. I only planted them four months ago. If you don't look after them properly when they're young, they'll never grow up to be strong.

SEBE: How will you pay the doctor if they get pneumonia?

HAYDAR: Nothing will happen to them.

SEBE: These are your children.

HAYDAR: They are as old as me when it comes to talking back. If they were my children, they would listen to me and care about what I have worked for. These trees are our future.

SEBE: Is that why you gave them away?

HAYDAR: She is my sister.

SEBE: You're killing yourself for those trees. Why not grow oak trees? You just plant them and let them grow. And the oak wood is stronger.

Silence.

HAYDAR: They look beautiful.

SEBE: They are the same as any other trees.

HAYDAR: Nobody sees there is a house here. The soldiers didn't notice our house the other day. Why? Because of how green and tall the trees are. The mulberries, the apple and pear orchard, but especially the silver birches. You'd think they touch the sky.

SEBE: They only missed us that one time. Maybe they weren't even searching houses that day.

HAYDAR: Still…

SEBE: What about in the winter? The trees won't hide us then. Anyway, they can just ask people for directions. Don't you think they have people in this village working for them?

HAYDAR: If we mind our own business perhaps they won't even come near us.

SEBE: We can't depend on that.

HAYDAR: We have to look after what we have. Is that too much to ask from my own family?

SEBE: The trees are beautiful. You have built this house, and I like it. But I don't think we've ever been happy here.

Pause.

Our family doesn't have a future here. Our children should study.

HAYDAR: Who studies in this village?

SEBE: It's time to move from here.

HAYDAR shouts.

HAYDAR: Where to?

SEBE: To the south. The land in the south is better and the winters are shorter. We can work in the factories. Tamer can work. The kids can study.

HAYDAR: You know nothing about the south!

SEBE: You always said that land is better there.

HAYDAR: I built this house with my own hands. I dug the stones to build it.

SEBE: I know that. We all worked hard, but if you were to say let's leave now, I wouldn't look back for one second.

HAYDAR: You've never appreciated what I've made.

SEBE: Haydar we are trapped in these mountains. We are not happy here. Can't you see that?

HAYDAR: How can you even think of leaving this paradise?

SEBE: It's your paradise not mine.

HAYDAR: I built it for you!

SEBE: How long are we going to live in poverty Haydar?

HAYDAR: We'll get by.

SEBE: Tamer is twenty. He should have his own family one day. Where would we put his family?

HAYDAR: We'll manage.

SEBE: I am scared that one day he will join them.

HAYDAR: Then let him.

SEBE: He is young. He thinks he can save the world.

HAYDAR: No one is going anywhere. Do you hear? No one!

He walks out.

SCENE 6

Two days later. It is evening. There is moonlight. TAMER sits on the floor outside the house, smoking. HAYDAR comes out. When TAMER sees him, he throws his cigarette away and sits up straight. HAYDAR sees the cigarette, but says nothing, and sits down next to him.

HAYDAR: Are you waiting for someone?

TAMER: Who would I be waiting for in this village?

HAYDAR: A girl, maybe?

TAMER: And which girl would that be?

HAYDAR plays with his hat. He is uncomfortable. He doesn't know how to begin. There is the sound of fireflies and frogs.

HAYDAR: It's mating time.

TAMER: What?

HAYDAR: Insects and frogs. They are breeding.

TAMER: Like people in this village.

51

HAYDAR: If it is God's will…

TAMER: God has nothing to do with it.

HAYDAR: If God wants to give people children, there's nothing to be done about that.

TAMER: There are ways to stop people breeding.

HAYDAR: Tell us if you know. You'll stop the poverty, then you'll be God.

TAMER: I'm not a doctor.

HAYDAR: In that case why do you speak like one?

TAMER: Maybe you're right. Maybe people here should breed like insects.

HAYDAR: Insects work hard. They make provisions for the future, as if they are going to live forever.

TAMER: Hmm. Right…

HAYDAR: Those insects die in the winter. But the new ones hatch with the warmth of summer. The sun boils their blood. People are the same. When they discover a new idea, they suddenly start looking at the world differently as if they had found the meaning of life. They buzz all summer like these insects. And then when the winter comes (*He makes a gun noise.*) bang they die.

TAMER: I am sure they are aware of their situation.

HAYDAR: It doesn't stop them working.

TAMER: What do you want Dad?

HAYDAR: Do you want to leave as well?

TAMER: Leave?

HAYDAR: Your mother wants us to leave this place. She wants to go to the city. Be a lady.

TAMER is silent.

TAMER: I think Mum is right.

HAYDAR: Your mother sits in the middle of this family like a goddess, and you all gather around her. I see you all talking, laughing with her and I think, what is it she shares with you. And I wonder why you don't love me.

TAMER: Dad we love her because she is our mother and we love you because you are our father.

Silence.

HAYDAR: I need your support Tamer.

TAMER: Leave me out of this.

Gets up and tries to leave.

HAYDAR: I am talking to you.

TAMER: You and Mum should sort out your own problems, and not involve us in them.

HAYDAR: Shhh. Do you hear?

TAMER: What?

HAYDAR: Just listen.

There are sounds of crickets, fireflies, frogs, water and trees in the background. TAMER is not interested but stays.

Can you hear the water, the trees, the frogs, the birds, and the insects? They are all in harmony on this long dark night. It's like heaven. Ahh! Peace. Your mother can not see all this. This is our house Tamer. It's your house. We must protect it.

TAMER: There was never peace in this land.

HAYDAR: If you want to get married, we'll build a new house.

TAMER: Dad, I don't want to work whole summers for other people and gain nothing in the end.

HAYDAR: This is the way we live here. Our animals have hay in the winter. That's something.

TAMER: It's not enough.

HAYDAR: It's enough for us to have milk, cheese and butter.

It's your bloody Comrades, isn't it? They do nothing but talk and walk around like a bunch of stray dogs with no jobs.

TAMER: Dad. The landowners get fatter and fatter from our blood and sweat.

HAYDAR: Didn't I tell you not to hang around with these communists?

TAMER: Maybe you shouldn't hang around with Baran either.

HAYDAR: Are you telling me what to do?

TAMER: He claims to be your friend, yet he's got me working in his field for a slave's wages.

HAYDAR: Are you telling me what to do?

TAMER: He is no good Dad. He wears a military uniform, he thinks he's a general!

HAYDAR: He is. He even has a gun.

TAMER: He's stupid. How can an illiterate man be a general?

HAYDAR: His business is his business.

TAMER: The man is a traitor and he is going to get killed one day.

HAYDAR: Who told you that? Have you joined them?

TAMER: Everybody knows he has a list of people who work with him.

HAYDAR: It's just talk. They want to take us to Russia for a better life? (*He laughs.*) Who's betraying who?

TAMER: They're not our enemies.

HAYDAR: They are the most dangerous enemies we have. All they want is to get you under their thumb.

TAMER: They are fighting for all the workers, and the peasants, for our future. I have to become a part of that.

HAYDAR: And then what? Where would you go, if you joined them?

TAMER: I don't know. They haven't said.

HAYDAR: Tamer, get this political rubbish out of your head. We are peasants and this is our village and this is our house. Are you not proud of our paradise?

TAMER: Maybe once it was a paradise. It should have been left alone.

HAYDAR: What do you mean?

TAMER: You know what I mean.

HAYDAR: We needed a house.

TAMER: Not here Dad, not here.

HAYDAR: There was nothing I could do. It was almost finished.

TAMER: I would have preferred to grow up in a barn, than live on this land.

HAYDAR: How about your mother and your sisters? Do you think they would like to live in a barn?

TAMER: I can't forget. I have never forgotten.

HAYDAR: Oh, come on son, be a man. They were just bones.

TAMER: (*Shouts.*) I am not afraid, all right.

HAYDAR: Then what is it?

TAMER: You…you were…nothing.

HAYDAR: We are all going to return back to earth one day.

TAMER: Where is my grandmother? And my two little uncles?

Silence.

HAYDAR: They have nothing to do with this.

TAMER: Was it them we saw when we were digging this ground?

HAYDAR: (*Shouting.*) You are unbelievable.

Silence. Becoming calmer.

They are nowhere.

TAMER: Nowhere…?

HAYDAR: They are in my grandmother's village. I had to work with my father that day. We saw people running towards us. They were running into the forest. People were shouting, telling us to run for our lives. We started running towards my grandmother's village. Then we saw the soldiers, just half a mile away. My father hid us behind a little bush and put his hand over my mouth to stop me from screaming. They were rounding everyone up from the village with guns. They forced them all to go into one of the houses. I saw my mother and brothers standing there. Then they went into the house. Suddenly I saw that the house was on fire. I never saw them again.

He is on the verge of crying.

There. They do not have a grave.

TAMER: Dad I am sorry. I thought Feride had found my grandmother's skull when we were digging here.

FERIDE is in a white dress. Enters the garden, holding skulls, her eyes are closed. She glides among the trees.

HAYDAR: I couldn't help myself.

TAMER: She was only a little girl. You almost killed her.

HAYDAR: I was angry.

FERIDE opens her eyes wide open, meaningless. The light fades from her.

TAMER: Everything here is an illusion.

HAYDAR: What? Don't you dare start talking like them. Trying to confuse me.

TAMER: What reality do you see Dad?

HAYDAR: I work hard, I dug this rocky ground, I built our house.

TAMER: Dad can't you see what's happening around you? (*Pause.*) There is life beyond this village.

HAYDAR: You are ungrateful. And how do you know these fancy words anyway?

TAMER: I read.

HAYDAR: There. You should be more grateful. I taught you how to read and write.

TAMER: I am grateful.

HAYDAR: Mockery is all I get in return. My father always said: 'Even if you feed a crow, it will still come and peck the eyes out of your corpse.'

TAMER: I don't know what else to say to make you understand.

HAYDAR: Don't join them. Work with me. Get married. Have a family.

TAMER: I don't want that.

HAYDAR: Your mum says that Kahraman's daughter likes you. She's nice, a beautiful girl. A bit short, but that's not a crime. I sometimes think that my midget uncle has something to do with that.

TAMER: Then I couldn't marry her, if she's my cousin.

HAYDAR: Marrying with a relative is good. They won't betray you.

TAMER: Mum is not your relative.

HAYDAR: True. Did you know I abducted your mother? She wanted to marry me, but her brothers forbade it. One night I waited for her by the river. It was a summer night like tonight. She came with all her clothes packed up into a bundle. She knew she wouldn't be allowed to go back home for a long time.

TAMER: It must've been tough.

HAYDAR: They were good days. I wasn't afraid of her brothers. Your mother loved me and that was enough. And now it's your turn. It doesn't have to be, what's her name?

TAMER: Who?

HAYDAR: Kahraman's daughter.

TAMER: We don't even know her name!

HAYDAR: If you love someone else then we should abduct her too. Like father like son.

TAMER: Dad, no.

HAYDAR: Then get engaged. People stay engaged for years. Finish your army service, we'll save some money, build a new house…

TAMER: I don't want that.

HAYDAR: What do you want?

TAMER: I want to do something that makes me happy. Something useful. I want to go far away from this little village, see different places. I want to change the wrongs that have been done to people, to us. I want to help people.

HAYDAR: You can do it here with our people.

TAMER: People here have forgotten how to laugh Dad. Their faces are painted with pain. I want to laugh with people. I want to meet real people and have real friends. I want to meet with those blood-drinking, child-snatching Caucasians. I don't want to spend all my life in a dead village. It's full of ghosts. It's hell, not heaven. If it's heaven to you, then you stay here, but let me live my own dreams.

HAYDAR walks towards TAMER. He raises his hand to beat him, but changes his mind. HAYDAR walks towards the silver birch trees. He touches the trees. He hugs them. There is a wind and the silver birch trees are shaking in the wind. We hear the wind and HAYDAR's sobbing.

SCENE 7

A week later. FERIDE comes from the bedroom. She is sleepwalking. HAYDAR is returning home late. He watches her. She passes him. HAYDAR goes after her.

HAYDAR: Feride!

Silence.

Feride! Where are you going?

FERIDE: There.

She points her finger in the direction of the waterfall beyond the silver birches.

HAYDAR: Where?

FERIDE: Mother calls me.

HAYDAR: Come inside Feride.

FERIDE: Look, she is sitting on the waterfall.

HAYDAR: Your mum is in bed.

She walks towards the waterfall. HAYDAR slaps her. She wakes up.

59

FERIDE: Ahh! What? What am I doing here? What did you do that for?

HAYDAR: Go back to bed.

FERIDE: Why is it so dark?

HAYDAR pulls her inside. She goes to her room. SEBE gets up from the sofa where she is sleeping, in the living room.

HAYDAR: She could have killed herself.

SEBE: Was she going to the waterfall again? She always has the same dream.

HAYDAR: Come to bed.

SEBE: Are you listening to me?

SEBE: Where were you?

HAYDAR: With Baran.

SEBE: What do you do there every night?

HAYDAR: We just talk.

SEBE: What do you talk about?

HAYDAR: Just things.

SEBE: We should take Feride to the shrine. She is getting worse.

HAYDAR: She is not the only child who walks in her sleep.

SEBE: But she's getting worse. It's not just the sleepwalking. I can't control her.

HAYDAR: We'll talk about it later.

SEBE: When it comes to your children, it's always later. Baran is more important than your family. Even those stupid trees are more important than us.

HAYDAR grabs her hair.

HAYDAR: Shut up, shut up!

SEBE: (*Sobs.*) Let go of my hair.

HAYDAR: Just shut up will you!

SEBE: That's it. I am leaving this house.

> *HAYDAR knocks SEBE against the wall. She screams. All the children run into the room. They behave as if they have seen this many times before. They try to separate HAYDAR and SEBE; one tries to pull HAYDAR back, while another tries to prise his fingers open so that he lets go of SEBE's hair, the third tries to pull the same arm away from SEBE's head. With his free arm, HAYDAR tries to punch SEBE. He hits and kicks the children too. During the fight, SEBE keeps talking as much as she can between hits, and the other dialogue overlaps.*

SEBE: (*To the children.*) You see what he's like?

FERIDE: What is it this time?

HAYDAR: Go back to your room.

SERAP: Dad please!

HAYDAR: I am going to kill her.

SEBE: You hear.

FILIZ: Mum.

HAYDAR: I told you not to nag. I told you go back to sleep.

FILIZ: Dad don't.

> *He punches and kicks SEBE over and over.*

Stop it. Please. Dad, please don't.

HAYDAR: Get away.

SEBE: Let him do what he wants. Do you want to kill me? Come on then.

> *He grabs her head and bangs it on the floor over and over. The children are shouting.*

FERIDE: Stop it. Stop it. Mum shut up!

The girls manage to separate HAYDAR and SEBE, and drag SEBE out to the orchard. She is still trying to talk back.

SEBE: I am leaving. And I'm taking the children with me.

FERIDE holds her mother's mouth and shuts the door.

HAYDAR: Who's stopping you? Get out of my house and don't come back again.

HAYDAR locks the door behind them. SEBE tries to push FERIDE out of her way so she can continue shouting at HAYDAR.

SEBE: What are you doing?

FERIDE: Shut up Mum.

SEBE: Don't tell me to shut up. I am your mother. I gave birth to you.

FERIDE: I wish you hadn't.

SEBE: I wish I hadn't too. You take after him. You all look like him.

SERAP: Speak quietly. He will come out if he hears you.

SEBE: Let him come.

FERIDE: Do you want him to hit us again?

SEBE: Do you think I like this?

FERIDE: Then why do you answer him back?

SEBE: You didn't have to join in.

FERIDE: If we didn't, he'd kill you.

FILIZ: Mum, I'm cold.

SEBE sits down on the floor and FILIZ lies on her lap.

SEBE: What are we going to do now?

FERIDE: I don't know. You should have thought about that before.

SEBE: All I said was that we should take you to the shrine.

FERIDE: How can a stone or a grave cure my sleepwalking? I am afraid of those graves anyway. You two can go to the shrine, but don't drag me there. Tie me to the bed.

Pause

SERAP: He's getting worse.

FERIDE: I'm tired Mum.

SERAP: Why don't we leave?

FERIDE: Shut up.

SERAP: You shut up.

FERIDE: Where would we go?

SERAP: To the city.

FERIDE: Dad would never let us.

SERAP: He just threw us out, didn't he?

FERIDE: You're dreaming.

SERAP: We can do it Mum.

FERIDE: We don't have any money.

SEBE: I'll ask your uncle to lend us some money.

FERIDE: How would we live? Where would we stay?

SERAP: We'll work. We'll work hard.

SEBE: We'll sleep on the streets if we have to. We'll be fine. Maybe Tamer will come too. Then we will all be together. Let's try to sleep now.

They sleep on the floor, hugging each other, trying to get warm.

After a while HAYDAR *opens the door and takes them in. He picks* FILIZ *up first and then* SERAP. FERIDE *and* SEBE *go in after him.*

SCENE 8

The following morning. SERAP *and* FILIZ *are in bed.* SEBE *enters. She is dressed nicely. She bundles up some food.*

SEBE: Come on Serap, get up. You too Filiz.

SERAP: Where are you going?

SEBE: Your father and I are taking Feride to the shrine.

FILIZ: But she didn't want to go.

SEBE: I'll ask Aunt Nare to look after you while we're gone.

FILIZ: I'll come too.

SEBE: No. You have to stay here.

SERAP: But what about our plan?

SEBE: We'll talk about it when we come back.

FILIZ: How did we get inside?

SERAP: You're going away. You're leaving us.

SEBE: Of course not.

FILIZ: Mum, don't go.

SEBE: You're being silly. We'll be back tomorrow. Don't tell Nare anything about our plan. It's our secret ok?

SERAP: (*Unhappy.*) Ok.

SEBE kisses both of them and walks out.

FILIZ: What if they're not coming back?

SERAP: She always does this. Why doesn't she stick to her decision?

FILIZ: Who will look after us?

SERAP: Let her leave if she wants to. We can look after ourselves. I know how to cook. Aunt Nare will teach me how to bake the bread and milk the cow.

FILIZ: Mum says Dad will bring a stepmother, and she won't be nice to us.

SERAP: Anything would be better than how things are now. I'm ready to leave. I even know the house we'll live in the city.

FILIZ: What do you mean?

SERAP: I've seen it in my dreams. Shall I tell you about it?

FILIZ: Yes.

SERAP: You have to close your eyes and listen carefully ok?

FILIZ: Ok.

SERAP: It has only one room, a really tidy one. One kitchen and one toilet. There are flowers in front of the windows. It's not that nice a house, but we make it nice by planting flowers around it. We wake up to the smell of jasmine every morning. There are shelves and cupboards and drawers all along the walls. All our clothes and bedding are in the drawers, so there is room to sit during the day. There are lots of shelves in the kitchen. We have lots of food, fresh fruit and vegetables so we're really healthy. Everything's nicely shelved. If something is missing, it gets replaced the next day. Mum wakes us up every morning, with breakfast. After we've eaten, Feride, Tamer and I go off to work. I help them to earn money and we save up. And when I can, I save some extra to buy books for both of us to go to school. You stay with Mum and help her with the housework. You have to take care of Mum and not let her come back here; otherwise Dad will kill her, ok?

FILIZ: Which city are we going to?

SERAP: Doesn't matter. Just so long as nobody knows us.

FILIZ: A big city!

SERAP: Yes. A city where we can do anything we want.

FILIZ: Will Tamer be with us?

SERAP: Of course.

FILIZ: Good. Do we have a bathroom?

SERAP: I didn't imagine the bathroom. No, we don't have a bathroom.

FILIZ: Where are we going to wash ourselves?

SERAP: In the kitchen. Like we used to.

FILIZ: Dad can build us a new bathroom.

SERAP: Dad won't be around, will he?

FILIZ: But all the other houses will have bathrooms.

SERAP: We'll heat the water and bathe in the kitchen, ok? Now let's go and have breakfast.

FILIZ: But you never have breakfast. Maybe we should wait for Aunt Nare.

SERAP: I am going to have breakfast today. And so are you. Come on.

They exit.

Act Two

SCENE 1

Winter. February 1980. Around four o'clock in the morning. The dog is barking. It is a windy night. Dark. SERAP and FILIZ are asleep in their bed. Because it is winter, the children are sleeping in the living room – the warmest room in the house. The bed is made from a mattress which has been put on top of benches which are used for seating during the day. SERAP hugs a radio playing at low volume while she sleeps. HAYDAR and two communists walk in: COMMUNIST 1 (male) and COMMUNIST 2 (female). They are dressed almost like soldiers, but don't have soldier's hats. They wear army boots. Their trousers and his beard are covered with snow. They sit on a bench beside SERAP and FILIZ's bed. The man's gun is in his lap. It is a big gun. SERAP begins to stir when she hears her father calling her name.

SERAP: Hmm…

SERAP opens her eyes. The gun is almost touching her nose.

HAYDAR: Serap wake up.

SERAP looks at their clothes, and realises they are communists. She smiles.

SERAP: I thought you were soldiers.

The COMMUNISTS sound and look very tired.

COMMUNIST 1: They don't have the guts to walk around at night.

He winks and smiles back to her.

HAYDAR: Maybe the soldiers are not that stupid.

SERAP: Dad!

HAYDAR: Come on Serap. Your mum is feeding the cows, so it's your job to prepare the breakfast.

SERAP: What time is it?

HAYDAR: It's almost five.

(*To the* COMMUNISTS.) Leave after you've finished eating.

COMMUNIST 2: We have to sleep for a while.

HAYDAR: Not here.

SERAP: Dad, their clothes are all wet. Let them stay today.

HAYDAR: Just do what I tell you. Take Filiz with you if you are afraid. The kitchen is dark.

SERAP is angry at the way her father treats her. She adopts a rebellious posture and an adult manner.

SERAP: I am not afraid. Let her sleep. She needs it.

SERAP takes a gas lamp and goes to the kitchen, but she hesitates.

COMMUNIST 2: You have a brave daughter. She is ready to fight.

HAYDAR: Is it her turn now?

COMMUNIST 1: Look Uncle, we don't force anyone to join us. They decide for themselves. Everyone is free to do whatever they want. We believe in democracy.

HAYDAR: I don't know what these fancy words mean, but if I am a free man then I can ask you to leave this house tonight. Can't I?

COMMUNIST 1: Why did you take us in then?

HAYDAR: The dog was barking.

COMMUNIST 1: Was that the only reason?

HAYDAR: You didn't go away.

COMMUNIST 2: Don't forget, we're fighting for you.

HAYDAR: You are like leeches. Once you stick on something, you suck out its life. Fighting for me! Who asked you to?

COMMUNIST 2: Are you against us Uncle Haydar?

HAYDAR: All I want is to be left in peace with my family. I am old enough to be your father. Why do you play games with me?

COMMUNIST 1: What about the games you're playing with us?

HAYDAR: What?

COMMUNIST 2: You know what he means.

HAYDAR: What? I don't play games. Not with anyone. You think I'd bother to play games with you? You think you're that important?

COMMUNIST 1: So you are not our friend?

HAYDAR: I have no reason to be your friend.

COMMUNIST 1: You prefer to be friends with people in high places.

HAYDAR: What do you mean?

COMMUNIST 1: We have the list.

HAYDAR: What list?

COMMUNIST 2: The list Baran left before he went on holiday with his forty virgins.

HAYDAR: I am friends with all of my neighbours, all of them. I mind my own business. I respect everyone and I expect the same thing in return.

COMMUNIST 2: Uncle Haydar, the snake that doesn't bite you isn't necessarily harmless. Don't shut your eyes to the people who are being bitten around you. If you think he was your friend, you are mistaken. Your name was on his list. He told us you were working with him as soon as he saw us. You owe your life to your son.

HAYDAR: You shouldn't have killed that man.

COMMUNIST 1: We don't kill randomly. We haven't killed you. (*Pause.*) But we're watching you. I hope we understand each other.

HAYDAR: I am not afraid of you.

COMMUNIST 2: Where is Tamer?

HAYDAR: I think you know where he is.

COMMUNIST 1: We'll find out anyway.

HAYDAR: You mean you don't know.

COMMUNIST 2: I thought we'd stopped playing games.

HAYDAR: You deserve to be in his place.

COMMUNIST 2: Is Tamer in trouble?

Pause.

HAYDAR: He's in prison. What are you going to do about that?

COMMUNIST 1: Don't you think we would know if he were in prison? Don't bullshit us.

HAYDAR: I'd rather he was in prison than with you.

COMMUNIST 1: We know where you sent him. We think you've sent Feride with him.

HAYDAR is angry.

HAYDAR: There was another operation two weeks ago. Didn't you hear? Obviously your intelligence is not as efficient as it should be, is it? They made us stand in the snow, in a line. Nobody was allowed to move, all day. Tamer, Feride, me and some other villagers; we were picked out and taken to the police station. They tortured my son. My daughter! Why? Can you tell me why?

COMMUNIST 1: There is no revolution without blood.

HAYDAR: If you're going to do something, do it properly. If you're going to have a revolution at least be professional about it.

COMMUNIST 2: Do you think we're doing this for fun? We walked in the snow for ten hours. We nearly froze to death.

COMMUNIST 1: Uncle Haydar, did they tell you what the charge was?

HAYDAR: Feeding you.

COMMUNIST 2: Is that the only reason?

HAYDAR: Of course that is the only reason. Look, we are poor people but still we share our food with people who knock on our door. This is our tradition. But show some respect, please. Choose your friends more carefully.

COMMUNIST 1: What are you talking about?

HAYDAR: One of your friends, a kid, from this village, gossiped to his fiancée on the phone about the people, about us. His neighbours! Apparently the police were looking for him. And when did he join you anyway? He is the laziest boy in this village. He can't even ride a horse. Don't you tell those people that the telephones are bugged? After two slaps, his fiancée gave the army everyone's names except the cows. Apparently me, my family and the other people who were taken with us were all members of your party.

COMMUNIST 2: These things happen. She's young.

HAYDAR: I know she is young, but I don't think you know what that means.

COMMUNIST 1: How do we know what you're saying is true?

HAYDAR: You think you are clever, but you don't even know what's happening among yourselves – let alone how to fight a revolution for us. You think I want my children to join you? I won't collect their bodies from the mountains. I won't let that happen.

COMMUNIST 2: That's enough.

HAYDAR: I don't like you. You are not right. You are not pure. You call your women comrades 'Sister', and then you sleep with them. That's disgusting. We don't have this kind of thing in our culture here. The word Sister has meaning for us. We don't just pluck words out of the air. If we call someone Sister, we mean it. Saving the poor? Saving people? And how on earth can you save people like us? You can't even save your own arses.

SERAP enters with a tray of breakfast and tea.

Now eat your breakfast and piss off, you fucking losers.

COMMUNIST 1 points his gun at HAYDAR.

COMMUNIST 1: You foolish old man. Do you want me to blow your head off?

SERAP puts the breakfast on the table. She walks towards COMMUNIST 1, standing between the gun and her father.

SERAP: Put the gun down, please.

COMMUNIST 1 lowers his gun. Looks at SERAP.

COMMUNIST 1: I'm sorry.

HAYDAR's voice trembles with anger.

HAYDAR: Let him shoot me. That's all they can do. Shoot people.

Beats both his knees and his head, he is hysterical.

Aah! Aah! I should have worked with Baran, then it would make sense to point a gun at me. (*He shakes his head.*) After I opened my door to you? Shared my food with you? You humiliate an honest man in front of his family. You…you are a piece of shit!

SERAP: Dad that's enough!

HAYDAR raises his hand to slap SERAP.

HAYDAR: Don't make me angry, I'll kill you.

SERAP: And is that all you can do? Beat me?

HAYDAR lowers his hand. SERAP looks at him with empty, cold eyes. She goes to the table and pours the tea. First she takes one to her father, then to the others.

Please. Come to the table. Eat.

Her father doesn't come to the table. She takes some bread, puts some cheese on it, and gives it to her father. She takes her tea and sits on her bed, watching the two COMMUNISTS, her father, and the guns.

SCENE 2

The following morning, in the same room. The COMMUNISTS are sleeping in SERAP and FILIZ's bed. SERAP is folding up the COMMUNISTS' jumpers and their socks, which have been dried carefully by the stove. They whisper, trying not to wake the two sleeping COMMUNISTS.

FILIZ: Who are they this time? Is Steel Hand here too?

SERAP: No, but I recognise the man. He came here once with Steel Hand last year.

FILIZ: Where is Mum?

SERAP: In the kitchen, baking bread. Go and have breakfast.

FILIZ: Are you not coming?

SERAP: No. You go.

FILIZ: You can't stay here on your own.

SERAP: Why not?

FILIZ: Because Dad won't like it.

SERAP: Who cares what he likes. Now don't be noisy. Go to the kitchen.

FILIZ sticks her tongue out at SERAP and leaves. SERAP sits on the bed. The guns are leaning against the wall next to her bed. She picks one of them up. It's too heavy for her, and almost the same height as her. She tries to put it on her shoulder like they do. COMMUNIST 1, who has woken up, watches her.

COMMUNIST 1: Be careful. It's loaded.

SERAP: Oh, I'm sorry. I didn't mean to wake you up.

COMMUNIST 1: Where is your father?

SERAP: He is in the mountains, chopping wood.

COMMUNIST 1 winks again.

COMMUNIST 1: Do you want to learn how to use it?

SERAP: Yes.

COMMUNIST 1: I'll teach you.

SERAP: When?

COMMUNIST 1: Whenever you like.

SERAP: Do you have anything lighter? Maybe a bit smaller than this.

COMMUNIST 1 laughs.

COMMUNIST 1: Of course we have. We have all sorts.

SERAP: Where do you get them?

COMMUNIST 1: You mustn't ask too many questions if you want to be a guerrilla.

SERAP: How else will I learn?

COMMUNIST 1: It's better if you know little in the beginning, in case they catch you. You don't want to tell them too much. But you will learn in time. If you don't get caught, that is.

SERAP looks at the guns.

SERAP: I am not afraid of torture.

COMMUNIST 1: You are a brave girl.

COMMUNIST 2 gets up.

COMMUNIST 2: I told you she is a fighter.

SERAP: So when can you teach me?

COMMUNIST 2: In the summer.

SERAP: So then I can go with you?

COMMUNIST 1: No. You will have to go to a camp for training.

SERAP: A camp?

COMMUNIST 1: You have to train.

SERAP: Will I be able to see my family?

COMMUNIST 2: The camps are in another country.

SERAP: Russia?

COMMUNIST 1: Perhaps. When we think you are ready for these mountains, you can come back and join us. Do you think you can manage to stay away from your mother for that long?

Thinks for a while, looks at her bed, sees FILIZ's T-shirt on the bed.

SERAP: Of course I can.

COMMUNIST 2: Good. Now, we lent Tamer some books. We think you still have them.

SERAP: I buried them. It was too dangerous to keep them around here after they were arrested. Feride is still at the police station. Did you know that?

COMMUNIST 1: So your father was telling the truth.

SERAP: Why would he lie?

COMMUNIST 2: Do you know why they are still holding Feride?

SERAP: I don't know. Nobody knows.

COMMUNIST 1: Is Tamer out?

SERAP: He went to Istanbul after he was released.

COMMUNIST 2: Feride is a brave girl. There is nothing they can charge her with.

SERAP: I'd like to believe that.

COMMUNIST 1: Believe it. Now do you think you can get those books for us?

SERAP: I can, but they are under snow, five feet down. It will take me a day, even more to dig them out. What if my father or the soldiers see me?

COMMUNIST 2: You don't have to, if you think you can't, but this is your first task.

Pause.

SERAP: When do you want them?

COMMUNIST 2: We will be back in three days.

SERAP: Ok.

COMMUNIST 2 goes to the window, and opens it.

COMMUNIST 2: Come here.

She balances the gun on SERAP's shoulder and aims outside. The gun is very heavy, it slips from her shoulder. She takes it back from her.

No, no hold it like this. Watch carefully.

She positions the gun on her own shoulder and pretends to pull the trigger. Then she puts the gun on SERAP's shoulder again and fires the gun. We hear a dog yelping, and then it stops.

SERAP: Mancho!

SERAP rushes out.

COMMUNIST 1: What have you done? She is only a little girl.

COMMUNIST 2: I am training her.

COMMUNIST 1: What are we going to tell her father now?

COMMUNIST 2: I didn't know that stupid dog was going to run across the yard.

COMMUNIST 1: Oh God.

COMMUNIST 2: Relax! It's only a dog.

COMMUNIST 1: That's not the point. You don't know these people. They treat their dogs like one of the family.

COMMUNIST 2: How was I supposed to know that?

COMMUNIST 1: Forget it. Get ready. We have to go.

They pick up their clothes and put their boots on. SERAP comes in. Her hands are bloody. She looks at her hands while she talks. Her lips are trembling, she is about to cry.

COMMUNIST 2: It was an accident. I didn't see him Serap. You have to believe me.

SERAP: It's my fault.

COMMUNIST 2: He was just a dog.

SERAP: He was innocent.

COMMUNIST 2: Yes, but he was still a dog. You have to be strong. These things shouldn't make you weak Serap.

COMMUNIST 1: You said you are not afraid of torture.

SERAP: I am not.

COMMUNIST 1: Imagine if they catch you, and they torture one of your friends by cutting a piece of flesh from his body every day. Will you talk to save him? If you talk, one of your friends might live, but five other comrades will die in his place. There is no time for weakness.

COMMUNIST 2: Come on, Serap be a brave girl.

SERAP: Yes, yes it was only a stupid dog.

Looks at her hands.

I'd better go and wash my hands.

She turns her back to them; we see the agony in her face, tears fall from her eyes. She walks slowly, tries to hide her face, walking rigid, without looking around her, avoiding their gaze so they do not see her tears. She leaves.

SCENE 3

Four days later. SERAP, SEBE and HAYDAR are in the living room again. There are books on the table. HAYDAR shouts.

HAYDAR: Tell me!

SERAP is silent.

I said whose books are they?

SERAP: They're mine.

HAYDAR: How did you get them?

SEBE: They are Tamer's books.

HAYDAR: What are they doing here?

SEBE: I told her to burn them, and she is going to, aren't you?

SERAP: I can't burn them when I know what's written in them, Mum.

SEBE: You've read enough.

HAYDAR: (*To SEBE.*) Did you know about this?

SERAP: They are good books. If you could read, you wouldn't burn them either.

HAYDAR: Where did you read them?

SEBE: She told me she was going to burn them.

She picks one of the books and looks at it.

SERAP: Have you ever heard of a country called Vietnam, Dad? They were people like us, and they won what they were fighting for. Isn't that incredible? Against America?

Short pause.

The comrades said they would come back to collect them in three days. They were supposed to be here last night. Something must've happened.

HAYDAR: Of course something happened. God knows where their carcasses are now. Don't you ever do things behind my back again.

He hits her with one of the books.

SERAP: Stop it!

HAYDAR: How did you become evil like this? None of my children talk back to me the way you do. I'll kill you…

He continues hitting her.

SERAP: I am not afraid of dying. If you touch me again, I swear, I will kill you.

HAYDAR throws all the books into the stove. Then walks out.

SERAP watches the fire, crying.

SCENE 4

Two days later. SERAP is in an empty school room. There is a SOLDIER at the door and a SERGEANT sitting in a chair in the middle of the room. SERAP has combed her hair nicely.

SERGEANT: So. Who is this beautiful young lady?

SERAP looks at the floor.

Answer me.

Looks at his face. She has no clue what is going on.

SERAP: Serap.

SERGEANT: Serap, can you tell me who combed your hair?

SERAP: I did.

SERGEANT: Are you sure that it wasn't one of the terrorists? One of your terrorist lovers…hmm? If you want to keep your beautiful hair, because you are very beautiful – and we don't want to hurt beautiful girls – then you'd better answer my questions. Now, tell me. When was the last time the terrorists came to your house?

SERAP: I don't know what you're talking about?

SERGEANT: Ok. You have a sister, don't you?

SERAP: Yes.

SERGEANT: And where is she now?

SERAP: Here. She is waiting in the other room.

SERGEANT: I am talking about your older sister, Feride.

SERAP: She is not here.

SERGEANT: Why not?

SERAP: (*Her voice is low.*) She has been taken to the police station.

SERGEANT: Who took her there?

SERAP: You took her there.

SERGEANT: You don't want to be taken there too, do you?

SERAP: No.

SERGEANT: Your other sister. Is her hair as beautiful as yours? Yes? Shall I cut her hair and maybe…her ear with it?

He touches her hair gently. He strokes and pulls it back tightly.

SERAP: Look, we don't know any terrorists and nobody comes to this village, but you.

He lets go of her hair.

SERGEANT: I'm going to let you go this time. But remember what I said about your sister.

SCENE 5

Two weeks later. Mid February. FERIDE and HAYDAR are sitting in the snow. They are eating bread and cheese. He watches her as she is having difficulty eating. She has been tortured.

HAYDAR: Did they feed you.

FERIDE: They gave me breakfast and something for dinner.

She looks away. Pause.

It was all right.

He doesn't ask anymore.

HAYDAR: Shall we go?

FERIDE: Can we rest a bit. I still have a headache.

HAYDAR: Did they...

FERIDE: Do you hear that?

HAYDAR: What?

FERIDE: The bird.

HAYDAR: What bird?

FERIDE: The Pepo bird.

HAYDAR: It's winter Feride. Pepo birds won't be here now.

FERIDE: It sounded like one.

HAYDAR: It must be a dog.

FERIDE: Why are they not here?

HAYDAR: Because the winter is so cold here, they go south.

FERIDE: How far is the south?

HAYDAR: Two months by horse. By bus, sixteen hours.

FERIDE: They fly that long?

HAYDAR: Yes he flies to find his sister.

FERIDE: Whose sister?

HAYDAR: Pepo bird's.

FERIDE: Tell me.

HAYDAR: I thought you didn't like me telling you stories.

FERIDE: I won't ask for one again.

HAYDAR: Once upon a time there was a brother and a sister called Keko and Pepo. One day their mother sent them to the forest to collect wild artichokes, so she could cook them for dinner. Pepo carried a bag, and her brother Keko carried a hoe. He collected the artichokes from the ground and gave them to his sister to put in the bag. She put every single artichoke into the bag. But there was a hole in it. And all the artichokes fell through it. After quite some time Keko said, 'I think that's enough for today, let's have a look how many artichokes we have collected.' But when he looked in the bag he discovered it was empty. He accused his sister of eating all the artichokes. She denied it, but he didn't believe her. She said to him 'If you don't believe me, open my tummy and see for yourself whether I ate them or not.' He was so angry to hear his sister lying to him that he picked up the hoe and ripped open her stomach. And he saw that she was telling the truth.

Feride! Feride!

She is very sleepy.

Are you listening?

FERIDE: Hmmmm?

HAYDAR: Keko didn't think that ripping open Pepo's tummy would kill her. When he saw that she was dead, he was sad and cried all the time. We'll both freeze if we stop walking. We're almost home. Here I'll carry you for a while.

He gives her a piggyback.

You'll feel better once you drink your mother's soup.

FERIDE: Am I heavy Dad?

HAYDAR: Yes, I feel like I am carrying a horse.

FERIDE: What happened after that?

She folds her arms around his neck.

HAYDAR: When he got home, his parents told him that he shouldn't cry any more because his sister had become a bird and had flown away. After hearing this, he begged to God day and night to turn him into a bird also, so that he could fly everywhere to look for his sister and ask for her forgiveness. After many days, God accepted his wish and turned him into a bird so that he could call out for his sister for ever and ever.

FERIDE: Pepo.

She lets go her arms around his neck. A cuckoo sings.

CUCKOO: Keko.

HAYDAR: Feride?

Silence.

CUCKOO: Pepo.

HAYDAR: Keko.

CUCKOO: Who killed?

HAYDAR in tears, his voice trembling.

HAYDAR: I killed.

He is by the door. FILIZ sees them.

FILIZ: Mum! Dad and Feride are here. Feride is here.

SEBE comes from the kitchen. She throws the ladle and tea towel, exited. HAYDAR enters. He is carrying FERIDE on his back, like a rucksack. She seems to be sleeping. HAYDAR goes towards SEBE.

SEBE: Is she sleeping?

HAYDAR: She has a headache.

SERAP and FILIZ are trying to wake her up.

Be gentle with her. She is sleeping. Bring her a nice pillow.

SERAP and FILIZ prepare the bed.

SEBE: Lay her on the bed. She must be so tired.

HAYDAR: She's gone Sebe.

SEBE: Don't be silly.

She laughs and cries at the same time.

She is just sleeping.

SEBE helps HAYDAR to take FERIDE's body from HAYDAR's back. SEBE realises that FERIDE is dead for certain. She collapses on her knees. HAYDAR arranges FERIDE on the bed. They all look down. SEBE strokes FERIDE's hair. SERAP takes FERIDE's shoes off. FILIZ holds FERIDE's hands. They all stroke her, trying to wake her up by kissing her hands, arms and her face. HAYDAR turns to the garden.

HAYDAR: (*Almost whispering.*) Will you accept my Feride too, tall silver birch trees? Will you embrace her, too?

SCENE 6

April 1980. HAYDAR is in the orchard planting flowers on FERIDE's grave.

HAYDAR: I don't know what flowers you like. I collected these from the mountains for you.

He plants some around the tree stump CEMIL cut. TAMER is sitting on the other side of the fence. HAYDAR can't see him. He talks to the tree stump.

Be my Feride's little baby boy. She'll take you. But you mustn't tire her. She has a headache.

He plants more flowers on FERIDE's grave. Now he talks to the grave.

It's a nice day. You were born on a perfect spring day. No. It was the beginning of June. Tamer gave me the news. He waited on the road for my return from the field till dawn. He ran towards me and said Dad, Dad, Mum has just had a little lamb, she cries like a lamb.

Pause.

I don't know what to say to you my little lamb.

TAMER is still on the other side of the fence. Lights a cigarette.

TAMER: You don't have anything to say.

HAYDAR is silent.

HAYDAR: When did you get here?

TAMER: Aren't you happy seeing me.

HAYDAR: You shouldn't be here.

TAMER: Do you think you can stop me from visiting my sister's grave?

HAYDAR: It's dangerous for you.

TAMER: Why didn't you let me know?

HAYDAR: Look son.

TAMER: I had a right to be at her funeral.

HAYDAR: Of course you did, but I was afraid that you would do something crazy.

TAMER: Bullshit.

HAYDAR: I was thinking of you.

TAMER: Bullshit. You've never thought about us.

HAYDAR: We shouldn't upset your mother now.

TAMER: Since when did you start worrying about Mum?

HAYDAR: What do you want?

TAMER: I want some answers.

HAYDAR: You give me some answers. It's all your fault.

TAMER: How can you say that?

HAYDAR: I told you stay away from them.

TAMER: I didn't join them!

> *Silent.*

> The trees won't bring her back Dad. And now you've added Feride to the collection, haven't you?

HAYDAR: How can you speak to me like that?

TAMER: If only I'd spoken to you like this before, Feride might still be alive now.

HAYDAR: Dear God. Dear God help me. I've raised snakes in my own house.

TAMER: Who is the little baby boy?

HAYDAR: Leave this house and my orchard at once!

> *SEBE enters.*

SEBE: What's going on here? Why are you shouting?

> *She's surprised to see TAMER.*

> Tamer when did you arrive?

> *She tries to hug him, but he doesn't cross the fence. She kisses him on both cheeks over the fence.*

HAYDAR: You've seen your mother, now leave.

TAMER: I'm going nowhere.

They attack each other.

HAYDAR: May God help me.

SEBE: Stop it.

HAYDAR: Stay away Sebe.

SEBE: You are going to kill each other. Stop it. Stop it. Not in front of Feride's grave.

Pause.

TAMER: Do you know there is a baby boy buried here Mum?

SEBE: What boy?

TAMER: Ask him.

SEBE: What is he talking about?

HAYDAR: Nothing.

TAMER: He is lying.

SEBE: (*Disapproving.*) Tamer!

What boy?

HAYDAR: It's nothing.

Looks at SEBE. She is not convinced.

In '38. During the trouble. (*He is almost delirious.*) We were trapped in a small cave.

SEBE: Yes, yes I know there was no water, no food…who was this baby boy?

HAYDAR looks only at SEBE, like a little boy looking to his mother for comfort.

HAYDAR: He kept crying. His mother tried to stop him by giving him her finger to suck, but he still cried from hunger. She put him under her cardigan, but you could still hear him screaming. We heard the footsteps above us. She looked at us, right into my eyes. Then she took her cardigan off and wrapped him up tightly in it. Like a shroud and pressed him tight to her chest. He didn't cry again. Her husband took the dead baby from her and didn't let go of him for three days. When the soldiers left, we buried the child here. She killed him to save me Sebe. I planted this tree on his grave then. Cemil cut it down. Evil has dogged us since that day.

SEBE: Why here?

HAYDAR: There was no better place than here. This is where the nameless people were buried after the last war.

SEBE: You knew there was a graveyard here all along.

HAYDAR: Yes.

Silence.

SEBE: Who were they?

HAYDAR: I'm not sure. People.

SEBE: I want you to make a nice gravestone for Feride.

HAYDAR: She likes the trees.

SEBE: I want her name written on stone. Or I will remove her body from this ground with my bare hands.

HAYDAR: We need to wait for the grave to settle.

SEBE: I don't want her to be nameless like the rest. Now leave me alone with my daughter. She wants some peace.

HAYDAR leaves. TAMER looks after him.

And when did you start smoking in front of your father?

He crosses the fence. Hugs his mother properly. Takes the flowers and plants them.

How long are you staying?

TAMER: I leave tonight.

SEBE: Where are you going?

TAMER: Istanbul.

SEBE: Are you with them?

TAMER: No.

SEBE: Good. I just baked some fresh bread.

TAMER: It's better if I don't stay.

SEBE: Give me your address.

> *TAMER takes a piece of paper and a pen from his pocket and writes his address. He gives the paper and some money as well. SEBE takes it. She says nothing.*

SEBE: Filiz. Serap. Come and say goodbye to your brother.

FILIZ: What?

SERAP: You've just got here?

FILIZ: You can't do that to us.

TAMER: I'll come back. I missed you.

FILIZ: We missed you too.

TAMER: Serap?

SERAP: What?

TAMER: See you soon.

SERAP: See you soon.

> *They hug and kiss each other. He kneels and kisses FERIDE's grave, then walks off.*

Don't forget us.

TAMER: I won't.

FILIZ: Promise?

TAMER: I promise.

FILIZ: He's gone.

Fade to black.

SCENE 7

Two days later. HAYDAR walks into the living room. It's dark. There is moonlight. It's quiet.

HAYDAR: Serap! Get me some water. I need to wash my feet.

Silence.

Sebe!

Silence. He turns the radio on. There is a play on.

The play's started. Black calf where are you. You are missing it all.

Silence. He gets up. Checks the house. Everywhere.

Sebe! Serap,

His voice drops.

Black calf!

He sits on the sofa. Holds the radio the way SERAP holds it. He gets up, goes to the orchard. Singing an old folk song:

> *Kir ciceklerini takma basina*
> *Kudret kalemini cekme kasina*
> *Beni aldatirsan doyma yasina*
> *Agla goz yasini sil mehlul mehlul.*

HAYDAR lies on his back and cries.

Come! Come and get me now! Help me! I have been waiting for such a long time.

There is a little wind, which shakes the leaves of the silver birch trees. We hear their rustling. Then we hear frogs, fireflies, owls and water.

SCENE 8

September 1980. City house. It's a small room, exactly as SERAP described. There are flip-up beds against the walls and there are drawers. One bed is down. SERAP and FILIZ have grown up a little. SERAP is tiding the house. FILIZ dances to lively music from a cassette player. SERAP watches her secretly while putting glasses and a jug of water on the table. FILIZ is tossing cushions in the air. SERAP gathers them.

SERAP: Filiz! I've just tidied the room.

FILIZ: Dance with me.

SERAP: No.

FILIZ: Why not!

SERAP: I can't.

FILIZ: Look. Watch me.

SERAP watches.

SERAP: How did you learn how to dance like this?

FILIZ: I learnt it from our new neighbour. Come on I'll teach you too.

FILIZ is teaching SERAP how to belly dance. SERAP starts dancing. This time they both toss the cushions happily in the air. SEBE comes in; she is surprised.

SEBE: What are you doing?

FILIZ: Mum look, I learnt how to belly dance.

SEBE: You what?

FILIZ: Watch!

SERAP stops, thinking she has done something wrong. FILIZ continues dancing. SEBE watches, at first surprised, but then with admiration. SERAP likes seeing her mother happy and dances with FILIZ. They both pull their mum to dance.

SEBE: No, no, not me.

FILIZ: Come on Mum.

SEBE: I don't know how to dance.

SERAP: Yes you do.

SEBE: I've never danced in my life.

> *They don't let go of her. TAMER walks in.*

> Tamer save me from these witches. They think I am young like them.

> *TAMER puts the shopping bags on the table. Laughing. He immediately takes the raki bottle out of the shopping bag and pours it. Takes a sip.*

> Tamer!

TAMER: You are young Mum.

> *He dances with his mother for a while. He tries to do belly dancing.*

SEBE: I called you for help.

TAMER: I am helping you.

SEBE: God help us all.

TAMER: Look Serap. Look what I can do.

SEBE: You are better than Filiz.

> *He dances with his mum and his sisters. TAMER takes a sip from his drink now and then. SEBE is totally lost among them; whenever she attempts to sit down TAMER and the girls don't let her. This is new to all of them and they can't stop laughing. The music stops. We hear the cassette player making a little noise and stop. They are tired of dancing and now they are on the floor, still laughing. HAYDAR walks in and watches them for a second. Black out.*

SCENE 9

A few minutes later. All are standing, except HAYDAR who is sitting.

SEBE: Filiz get your father some water.

HAYDAR: It's all gone Sebe.

SEBE takes the water from FILIZ.

SEBE: Have some water.

HAYDAR: They burnt my heaven.

TAMER: Who? Dad who did it?

HAYDAR: Soldiers.

SEBE: Nare and Cemil. Where are they? Has anyone died?

SERAP: Dad is Ayse all right?

HAYDAR: Calm down Sebe. You are scaring the children. Nobody died this time. They gave us one week's warning.

SEBE: What have you done with the animals?

HAYDAR: What could we do in a week? Cemil and I took the animals to the town, but everyone was trying to sell their animals. So eventually we sold them for next to nothing. They'd started burning the houses by the time we got home. Cemil's brother took Nare and Ayse with him to the South. They have a relative there. Cemil has followed them, and I've come here. If that's ok with you all.

He looks at SEBE. She acknowledges with her head.

TAMER: Did they burn our house?

HAYDAR: Yes.

SEBE: Everything?

HAYDAR: They didn't touch the orchard.

Are you drinking that shit again? (*Meaning the raki on the table.*)

93

TAMER: Some things never change, do they?

HAYDAR: It's forbidden.

TAMER: No it's not.

HAYDAR: You are committing a sin.

TAMER raises his glass to his father but doesn't drink yet.

TAMER: 'To share one grape among friends.'

TAMER pours a drink for his father.

I don't believe in God, but then neither do you.

HAYDAR: I have my own beliefs.

TAMER offers the glass to his father and quotes:

TAMER: 'Others turn to Mecca to pray,
    I turn to you.'

HAYDAR: (*Laughing.*) Son of a dog.

TAMER: (*Laughing.*) If I were you, I wouldn't say that.

Mum?

SEBE: Oh no. Not for me.

HAYDAR is gentle with her for the first time.

HAYDAR: Come on Sebe, drink with me. Let's all have a drink.

SEBE: What are we celebrating?

HAYDAR: No children died this time.

SEBE: I wish that was true.

HAYDAR: I'll go back and do what I promised for Feride. But when things get calmer. I promise.

TAMER hands drinks to everybody, except FILIZ.

FILIZ: What about me?

HAYDAR: Give some to my black calf, but not much.

SEBE: Haydar please, it's not good for her. This is not the time for celebration.

HAYDAR: Sebe I don't usually touch this stuff, you all know that. And when do we ever celebrate anything anyway, ha? No, today I am going to drink. This time we were given one week's notice. Things are changing. And I am going to drink to my unburned orchard.

TAMER pours a small drink for FILIZ and hands it to her.

SERAP: I missed our mulberry garden!

FILIZ: At least we don't have to pick them for every person who passes by. God I hated that.

HAYDAR: You won't understand it now black calf. But you will, one day.

FILIZ: Understand what? We were feeding every single stranger passing by. 'Oh, no please don't go without tasting our apricots. Please have some mulberries and some pears.'

HAYDAR: I wanted to create a heaven and offer its fruits to everybody.

SERAP: You did Dad. You created a heaven for every body and every soul. And I'm sure the fruits from that heaven reached every single person who deserved to taste them.

HAYDAR: She is a devil. A sweet little devil with a little nose.

TAMER: Dad?

HAYDAR: What?

TAMER: If the silver birches are still there, you can still visit them every summer. I'll come with you if you want.

HAYDAR: What do you say Sebe? You can come with us too.

SEBE: We'll see.

He looks at everybody.

HAYDAR: What are we waiting for then? Come on! To life.

To us.

To my heaven.

His eyes gets watery, his voice trembles.

To my constantly disturbed heaven.

To my little Feride!

All raise their glasses. Then bow their heads, thinking of FERIDE. We see FERIDE, flowers in her hair. She sits on the (little boy's) tree stump. SERAP looks up at FERIDE. They smile at each other. FERIDE disappears, but SERAP continues to smile.

SERAP: To the future!

HAYDAR: To the future, to our great unknown future.

All drink.

The End.